"Burke's stories and articles from theooze.com are ma[de] the reader perceptive insight into the myriad issues [in] culture. Whether you are a regular church attender fro[m] stepped inside a church in years, this book will facilit[ate] we dream about the church into the twenty-first centu[ry],.

—JOEL VESTAL, founder and president, ServLife International, Inc.; author of *Dangerous Faith*

"*Out of the Ooze* is a collection of the writings from various exiles, mystics, poets, and dreamers of the postmodern church. As such, it gives eloquent voice to the rich litany of interests and concerns of a generation. Eclectic, edgy, intelligent, and generative, this is a book that will help the reader better understand the ardent search for a place to stand that so characterizes the Western church in our time."

—AL HIRSCH, coauthor of *The Forgotten Ways* and *The Shaping of Things to Come*; founding director, Forge Mission Training Network

"*Out of the Ooze* is theology of the people, by the people and for the people. Having sifted through hundreds of thousands of web contributions to theOOZE.com, Spencer Burke has selected a few choice offerings, inviting us to encounter the concerns, wonderings, and awakenings of real people seeking to live faithfully in the way of Jesus in these times. No doubt there will be points of dissonance, but *Out of the Ooze* will compel you to focus and refocus your vision of the living gospel with the hope of a new kingdom resonance."

—DWIGHT J. FRIESEN, assistant professor, Mars Hill Graduate School

"When ancient stone walls were built, there was no mortar or mix to secure the rocks. Each rock was set in place and then tapped by a hammer. When the sound was 'right,' the next stone was wedged in place until its sound was right. *Out of the Ooze* proves that Spencer Burke has mastered this ancient craft, but his medium is blogs, posts, and paragraphs, not rocks. Each contribution sounds a perfect pitch of selection and placement. Listen carefully and you will hear the groundswell of new sounds and structures being built."

—LEONARD SWEET, Drew University, George Fox University, www.wikiletics.com

"*Out of the Ooze* is written by people who care very much about the church but are not naive about the church. They care enough to speak, to question, and also to offer hope. These are fresh voices that need to be heard. You will not necessarily agree; you might even get agitated. Still, listen to these voices. They call us to reflect on our church practices and challenge us to be a church that blesses the world in Jesus' name."

—KURT FREDRICKSON, DMin, director, Doctor of Ministry Program, Fuller Theological Seminary

NAVPRESS
DELIBERATE

From the very beginning, God created humans to love Him and each other. He intended for His people to be a blessing to everyone on earth so that everyone would know Him (see Genesis 12:2). Jesus also taught this over and over and promised to give His people all they needed to make it happen—His resources, His power, and His presence (see Matthew 28:20; John 14:12-14). NavPress Deliberate takes Him at His word and stirs its readers to do the same—to be the children of God for whom creation is groaning to be revealed. We have only to glance through the Bible to discover what it looks like to be the blessing God has intended: caring for the poor, orphan, widow, prisoner, and foreigner (see Micah 6:8; Matthew 25:31-46; Isaiah 58); and redeeming the world—everyone and everything in it (see Colossians 1:19-20; Romans 8:19-23).

NavPress Deliberate encourages readers to embrace this holistic and vibrant Christian faith: It is both contemplative and active; it unites mystery-embracing faith with theological rootedness; it breaks down the sacred/secular divide, recognizing God's sovereignty and redemptive work in every facet of life; it dialogues with other faiths and worldviews and embraces God's truth found there; it creates culture and uses artistic ability to unflinchingly tell the truth about this life and God's redemption of it; it fosters a faith bold enough to incarnate the gospel in a shrinking and diverse world. NavPress Deliberate is for everyone on a pilgrimage to become like Jesus and to continue His work of living and discipling among all people.

Become what you believe.
The NavPress Deliberate Team

OUT OF THEOOZE

Unlikely Love Letters to the Church from Beyond the Pew

SPENCER BURKE, CURATOR

OUR GUARANTEE TO YOU

We believe so strongly in the message of our books that we are making this quality guarantee to you. If for any reason you are disappointed with the content of this book, return the title page to us with your name and address and we will refund to you the list price of the book. To help us serve you better, please briefly describe why you were disappointed. Mail your refund request to: NavPress, P.O. Box 35002, Colorado Springs, CO 80935.

The Navigators is an international Christian organization. Our mission is to advance the gospel of Jesus and His kingdom into the nations through spiritual generations of laborers living and discipling among the lost. We see a vital movement of the gospel, fueled by prevailing prayer, flowing freely through relational networks and out into the nations where workers for the kingdom are next door to everywhere.

NavPress is the publishing ministry of The Navigators. The mission of NavPress is to reach, disciple, and equip people to know Christ and make Him known by publishing life-related materials that are biblically rooted and culturally relevant. Our vision is to stimulate spiritual transformation through every product we publish.

ISBN-13: 978-1-60006-213-1
ISBN-10: 1-60006-213-X

Cover design by The DesignWorks Group, Charles Brock, www.thedesignworksgroup.com
Cover image by The DesignWorks Group
Creative Team: Caleb Seeling, Reagen Reed, Arvid Wallen, Pat Reinheimer

Some of the anecdotal illustrations in this book are true to life and are included with the permission of the persons involved. All other illustrations are composites of real situations, and any resemblance to people living or dead is coincidental.

Unless otherwise identified, all Scripture quotations in this publication are taken from the HOLY BIBLE: NEW INTERNATIONAL VERSION® (NIV®). Copyright © 1973, 1978, 1984 by International Bible Society. Used by permission of Zondervan Publishing House. All rights reserved. Other versions used include: the *New American Standard Bible* (NASB), © The Lockman Foundation 1960, 1962, 1963, 1968, 1971, 1972, 1973, 1975, 1977, 1995; the *Holy Bible, New Living Translation* (NLT), copyright © 1996, 2004. Used by permission of Tyndale House Publishers, Inc., Carol Stream, Illinois 60188. All rights reserved; and the *King James Version* (KJV). The author's paraphrases are marked PAR.

The article "Detoxing from Church" first appeared on www.theofframp.org.
The article "The Skinny on Postmodernity" by Andrew Jones was originally presented as a lecture at Golden Gate Baptist Theological Seminary in 1999.

Out of the ooze : unlikely love letters to the church from beyond the
pew / Spencer Burke, curator.
    p. cm.
Includes bibliographical references.
ISBN-13: 978-1-60006-213-1
ISBN-10: 1-60006-213-X
1. Christianity--21st century. 2. Postmodernism--Religious
aspects--Christianity. 3. Emerging church movement. I. Burke, Spencer.
II.

BR121.3.O98 2007
269--dc22

2007027826
Printed in the United States of America
1 2 3 4 5 6 7 8 / 11 10 09 08 07

FOR A FREE CATALOG OF NAVPRESS BOOKS & BIBLE STUDIES,
CALL 1-800-366-7788 (USA) OR 1-800-839-4769 (CANADA).

To Dave and Jan Coleman

You have encouraged me to have the wisdom of a serpent but be harmless as a dove. You are a constant example that the church can be "both/and" and that there is beauty within the established church and also beyond. Thank you for your love and support.

CONTENTS

WONDERING   147

RESPONDING   175

ACKNOWLEDGMENTS

There are many people I've served alongside professionally in ministry who have nurtured my voice, encouraging me to develop my unique perspectives, opinions, and beliefs. Kenton Beshore, Keith Page, Todd Proctor, and all the staff at Mariners Church and Rock Harbor Church gave me the space for open and honest dialogue, continuing to be friends and fellow ministers, to be willing to talk through ideas, and to give me the freedom to explore the topics in this book.

TheOOZE.com community is a source of inspiration and hope for me and the church. Thanks to all who come to the website whether just to visit or to dig in and interact. To those who write articles, read articles, post comments, meet on- and offline, and gather annually at our learning party, Soularize, your interest in each other, your faith, and the church is the heartbeat of TheOOZE.com. Thanks for keeping it alive.

To the team of volunteers who actually run TheOOZE.com and all the related effort it takes to support a community like this, you have invested part of your lives in TheOOZE and I am forever grateful: Malcolm Hawker, Jim and Tammy Schoch, Lydia Schoch, Shayna Metzner, Mike DeVries, Sarah Taylor, Jordan Cooper, John O'Keefe, Alan Hartung, Tim Hill, Julie Kennedy. I also want to acknowledge those who were part of the early conceptualization, planning, and creation of TheOOZE: David Trotter, Anita Roach, Ray Majoran, Mark Doud, Dana Hogan, Tim Taber, Matt Palmer, Kataro Shimagori.

Another team made this book a reality: Caleb Seeling and the NavPress Deliberate team of editors. Caleb, I love your vision to reach beyond the boundaries of traditional subjects and voices. David Sanford, Rebekah Clark, and Sanford Communications helped me hone in on the best of the millions of ideas that run through my brain, giving reality to this book and the discovery of emerging voices. And thanks to the team of writers who helped me pull all the pieces together and gave shape to this work: Colleen Pepper, Mike DeVries, and Lisa Burke.

To my wife, Lisa, thank you for the all the learning, rethinking, and rebudgeting throughout this adventure called TheOOZE.

INTRODUCTION

There are certain things that usually only those who truly love you will tell you. Like when you've got that little piece of parsley stuck in your teeth or your zipper is down. Or more important things, like when it's time to move on from a harmful relationship or when you're pushing your kids so much that you're discouraging instead of encouraging them.

I might resist or resent it when my wife, Lisa, tells me my driving is too aggressive or that I need to rethink the purchase of my next high-end techno gadget. I might call her critical or ignore her. Or I might give thoughtful consideration to her suggestion. Often how I receive her words depends on the day I've had and my frame of mind. Sometimes it depends on how she's delivered the message. Usually, I need to hear and not ignore Lisa's words. We all need to hear our friends' and family's words of caution and care, their reminders and encouragement, and their shared hope and joy too.

It's true in our personal lives, and it's true in our community as well. For me, that means the church. I was a professional pastor for twenty-two years, and I sometimes resisted and sometimes resented people asking tough questions and raising warning flags. One day I realized that the people questioning the church and the systems of faith I supported were not all bad, angry people with a chip on their shoulder or a personal agenda. As with my wife, how I received their input depended on my frame of mind and how they raised the issue — but I also needed to hear their words. I believe the larger church community needs to hear them too, keeping an open mind and a willingness to hear the truth that we, up to now, might have been deaf to.

In 1998, I decided to launch TheOOZE.com as a place where people could come and share their questions, longings, and musings about the body of Christ. My desire was to create a place where honest and transparent dialogue about faith, culture, and ministry could happen.

Since that time, TheOOZE.com has grown to over two hundred and fifty thousand visitors a month from more than one hundred countries around the world. Who are these people? They're people who love the church and desperately want to see her become the essential, life-giving community that God designed her to be. They come from a wide variety of traditions, viewpoints, and cultures.

Some visit often. Others only for a season, but almost all come with one goal in mind—to try to understand more about what it means to be a follower of Jesus in a rapidly changing, postmodern world. What is the church? What role does the church play in the larger culture around it? How should the church engage that culture?

A while ago, a friend showed me a business card with two Chinese symbols on it. "This is the Chinese word for 'crisis,'" he explained. "It's made up of two distinct characters that are in fact words on their own. One is the symbol for the word *danger*. The other is the symbol for the word *opportunity*."

I've never forgotten that conversation. I think we can safely say that the church today is in crisis. The institution as we have known it is clearly in danger, yet with that threat comes opportunity. As the modern church struggles to survive, we can either attempt to defend and maintain the status quo at any cost, or we can see the situation as an opportunity to go beyond where we've been and explore new ways of doing—and, perhaps more importantly, being—the church.

In 2001, I wrote a book called *Making Sense of Church: Eavesdropping on Emerging Conversations about God, Community, and Culture.* In it I tried to bring understanding between those who would call themselves 'emerging' and the rest of the church. I wanted to help Christians understand the possible sources of the tension in their faith communities and the areas where changes were needed.

In many ways, this book is a continuation of that work. It provides more insight into the issues and challenges facing the church, as well as a healthy dose of hope for the future. But while *Making Sense of Church* drew heavily from the exchanges happening on TheOOZE message boards at the time, the following pages are drawn instead from a sampling of TheOOZE articles.

One of the great things about TheOOZE is that it allows everyone to be an author. Each week, we get dozens of new articles submitted from all kinds of intriguing personalities. Some are voices we've heard before, but most are completely unknown to us. They're just ordinary people with a point to make or a question to ask or an idea to share. TheOOZE gives them a platform and an opportunity to be heard.

A few weeks ago, I was doing some online gaming with my son, Alden. We were in the heat of a game when I suddenly realized how strange the whole situation was — and how indicative it was of the new social reality. There we were, hanging out online with perfect strangers. We didn't know who these people were, where they were from, or anything about them. We didn't know if we were playing with a thirty-four-year-old software engineer in Silicon Valley, or a ten-year-old kid from Arkansas. And yet, there we were, taking these people's advice and trusting them for our next move.

Like it or not, the world has changed. In the past, we gave people our respect and attention because of their education, experience, or position. We listened to them largely because of who they were and what credentials they held. Similarly, we often rejected ideas not because they were untrue but because we didn't like the person delivering them.

But with the advent of blogging and online conversation, wisdom is no longer the exclusive property of those with degrees, titles, or even certain experiences to their credit. The Internet has democratized the conversation. Today ideas are accepted or rejected not because of the position or power of the deliverer but based upon the integrity of the idea itself. Is it insightful? Is it filled with passion and wisdom? Does it harmonize with the way of Jesus?

Perhaps one of the least explored benefits of online conversation is the way in which it can move us beyond our preconceived prejudices and transcend our biases.

The reality is that this book was not written by experts. We didn't ask these people to submit material for a book of essays or tell them what topics to write on. They just showed up at TheOOZE one day and started throwing ideas around. When we saw the things they were saying online, we thought it would be good to share them offline, as well, to give their ideas broader exposure. Some ideas we agreed with; some we didn't. But we thought they were worth sharing just the same.

I'm reminded of the graffitied walls I often see near my home in southern California. No one really asks people to come and spray paint on their walls. It just happens. To some, it's ugly. Bits of poster here, spray-painted tags there, parts of an old mural over there. But look closer, and you can find great beauty as well.

Several years ago, I actually started taking pictures of these walls. By framing small pieces through the lens of my camera and playing with lighting and composition, I found I was able to come up with some really powerful images. At one point, I was even asked to display my work at a well-known gallery.

I can still remember going to the opening of the show and hearing people ooh and ah over my photos. The whole night was so surreal. The wine, the cheese, the black turtlenecks. Every image was beautifully framed and perfectly lit on the pristine gallery walls. There were little cards for each piece explaining the fine technical details of the image and my inspiration for capturing it.

Throughout the night, people kept coming up and saying things like, "These are fantastic. Why haven't we seen these before?"

But that's just it. They could have seen those images before if they had wanted to. We were, after all, looking at pictures of graffiti from the street. Had they gone down the right alley, the raw material would have been right there in front of them. But that was exactly the problem. People didn't see the beauty until someone framed it for them and lit it properly.

In a sense, that's what I'm trying to do with this book. I want to give people an opportunity to hear the heart of the tagger—the person who no longer fits in the modern church and is instead wandering down less traveled streets in pursuit of a different Christian experience. The articles in this book aren't acts of vandalism. They're love letters to the church and postcards back to the rest of culture.

As for me, I'm just the curator of the collection. My role isn't to agree or disagree with the ideas; I simply want to frame and present them.

As you read through the following pages, you'll notice that the articles have been arranged not by topic or theme or even issue but by season of life. In Ecclesiastes 3 we read, "There is a time for everything, and a season for every activity under heaven" (verse 1). Truly, there is "a time to plant and a time to uproot . . . a time to tear down and a time to build . . . a time to keep and a time to throw away" (verses 2,3,6). For many of us in the emerging church conversation, the challenge is knowing when to engage in each of those activities. And in the meantime, we awaken, rethink, experience, and wonder. Eventually, of course, we must also respond. We need to frame our journey in such a way that others can understand it and in some way, engage it.

I've heard it said that it takes seven or eight years to mature, develop, and process new thoughts and emotions about your life—where you've been and where you're going. That's about how long TheOOZE.com has been around, and that's why this book can be written today. As you read it, you'll get a sense that the writers are processing their new thoughts and feelings about their faith and the church. Perhaps wherever you are on your journey, you can identify with one of the seasons in this compilation. It's my desire that this book will help you not only to come to a deeper appreciation of the issues being discussed in the emerging church movement but also give you a greater love for those whose spiritual journey has taken them outside the modern church and, in many cases, beyond the pew.

SPENCER BURKE

AWAKENING

I DON'T KNOW ABOUT YOU, but if I had my life to live over, I'd probably do a few things differently. I'd still marry my wife, Lisa, and I wouldn't trade being a dad for anything, but I probably wouldn't have stood in the middle of Marconi Avenue to take that photograph when I was seventeen. Don't get me wrong; it was a great shot. But looking back, getting hit by a car and spending the next six months learning to walk again was kind of a steep price to pay for it.

Yet that's the dynamic nature of life. As things happen to us or we get new information or as time simply passes, we begin to see things differently. Sometimes the change in perspective happens almost imperceptibly. We get up every day, put on clothes, go to work, and, somehow, in the midst of that ordinariness, change happens. Other times we experience a dramatic, Paul-on-the-road-to-Damascus-type conversion, complete with a self-inflicted how-could-I-have-ever-thought-that slap to the head. Picture the guy who thought New Coke was a great idea, or the choreographer who thought Justin Timberlake should reach over and help Janet Jackson with her costume change at the Super Bowl.

A few months ago, I did a radio show interview about my last book project, and the host could hardly wait to ask me if I'd changed my mind about anything I'd written. To be fair, I talked about some pretty controversial things in the book, so it wasn't a completely ridiculous question, yet I could tell the guy was disappointed when I didn't recant then and there. Instead, I said, "You know, if I'm not a little embarrassed about the things I said yesterday, then I haven't learned anything today." And the thing is, I really think that. Believe me, I said an awful lot of things from the pulpit over the years that I certainly wouldn't say now. But I thought they were true and helpful words at the time, so I said them. I did the best I could with the information, experience, and understanding I had at the time.

Of course, one of the things the emerging church movement has often been criticized for is being overly negative. And truthfully, there is a lot of critiquing and criticizing on TheOOZE. But I would argue that it's critiquing for a purpose. It's criticism that's born out of a desire to see things change for the better. It's as much a calling forth as it is a calling onto the carpet.

For many OOZE-ers, this critiquing phase leads to a period of self-examination and an awareness that not all of the modern church's failings are someone else's fault. Indeed, we all have to take some responsibility for where we are today and for the circumstances in which the church finds itself. As Dr. Phil likes to say, "You're getting something out of this." Why is the church the way it is? Because, in large part, we've allowed it to be. We got something out of it.

In this first section of articles, you'll hear OOZE-ers as they come to grips with this reality and begin to see themselves as part of both the problem and the solution.

I'M SORRY

One Christian Apologizes to the World

STEVE CONRAD / APRIL 14, 2005

I'm sorry.

What else can I say? No excuses. No rationalizations. No trying to explain my point of view. Just, I'm sorry.

I can face facts. The fact is that many people look at the church and Christians with disdain and disregard. We are generally politely tolerated, sometimes laughed at, and occasionally viewed as a menace to society. And if I'm honest with myself, I will admit that in many cases we deserve the treatment we get. That's why I'm writing. I am just one man. I would never presume to speak for the millions of Christians around the world or the church as a whole, but, speaking for myself, I confess that I have lived a life that has all too often given a bad name to Christianity. I grew up in the church and have seen how the church can do amazing things in the lives of people. But I have also seen how the Christian community can devour its own and how it can turn its back to a hurting world and suffering people. I see what Jesus intended the church to be, and I see what we have become instead. I perceive a huge divide between what we are called to be and what we truly are.

Again, I'm sorry.

The reasons people have for being disenfranchised with the church are varied. Some cite the historical mistakes that Christians have made — how the church has frequently persecuted those that are deemed offensive and has promoted a culture of intolerance. Others are turned off by the examples of Christians that they see in our culture—public figures who have grossly misused their platform, often for personal gain. Still others have been personally hurt by the church or Christians in their lives, suffering at the hands of people who are supposed to love them. All of these factors result in a culture in which many consider Christians to be negative, preachy, hypocritical, and judgmental people. Christians are known for the things that we oppose, not the things that we embrace and hold dear.

More and more, Christianity is becoming marginalized in our culture. Most people believe that Christian faith is irrelevant to the realities of life. Between work, families, and a wide range of entertainment options, there just isn't much room left in our world for faith. And, as Christians, we aren't giving any compelling reasons to think otherwise.

It's not supposed to be like this. As I read Scripture, I see that Jesus has called us to be shining lights and messengers of hope. But we have abdicated our role and covered up our lights. We stand by and watch as people struggle with poverty, depression, and dysfunction. We see people oppressed and killed around the world, and do little or nothing. It seems we're more concerned about whether we can display the Ten Commandments on a courtroom wall than whether we care for those around us. And that's not how Jesus has called us to live.

I'm sorry.

 THE EVIDENCE

Throughout history, the church has brought much shame to itself. From the Crusades to the Spanish Inquisition, from the Salem witch trials to the bombing of abortion clinics, much evil has been inflicted on the world in the name of Christianity. The church has abused its power and sought to gain control through unconscionable acts. Where Christ called the church to be a source of light and hope, it has too often become a source of pain and suffering. In more recent times, the church has become the voice of judgment and intolerance. For an institution that is supposed to be defined by love, we certainly don't show it. Righteous indignation we have plenty of, but love, grace, and compassion are often in short supply.

A recent Barna poll asked individuals who would not consider themselves Christians to rank various social groups from most favorable to least favorable. The different groups included categories like military officers, ministers, evangelicals, Democrats, Republicans, real-estate agents, TV performers, lawyers, lesbians, and prostitutes. Out of the eleven groups specified in the poll, evangelicals ranked tenth, behind lawyers, lesbians, and Republicans, but finishing ahead of prostitutes. Only 22 percent of the respondents gave evangelicals a favorable rating. And while some may believe that the widespread negative view of evangelical Christians is an undeserved stereotype, I don't think we can deny that there are many reasons why we have earned our less-than-favorable status.

A quick search of the Web yields pages of quotes from various authors, comedians, and religious and political leaders which give voice to concerns many have about Christianity and the church. Here's a sampling:

- "The careful student of history will discover that Christianity has been of very little value in advancing civilization, but has done a great deal toward retarding it." —Matilda Joslyn Gage
- "It is usually when men are at their most religious that they behave with the least sense and the greatest cruelty." —Ilka Chase
- "One would like to believe that people who think of themselves as devout Christians would also behave in a manner that is in according with Christian ethics. But pastorally and existentially, I know that this is not the case, and never has been." —Richard John Neuhaus
- "The trouble with born-again Christians is that they are an even bigger pain the second time around." —Herb Caen
- Bart: What religion are you? Homer: You know, the one with all the well-meaning rules that don't work out in real life. Uh . . . Christianity. —*The Simpsons*

* "If Christ were here now there is one thing he would not be—a Christian." —Mark Twain
* "I'm not often so comfortable in church. It feels pious and so unlike the Christ that I read about in the Scriptures." —Bono
* "I like your Christ; I do not like your Christians. Your Christians are so unlike your Christ." —Gandhi

Unfortunately, instead of love being the defining characteristic of a Christian, today a Christian is often best defined as a hypocrite. Philosopher Bertrand Russell wrote a book entitled, *Why I Am Not a Christian*. The primary reason that he cites is the hypocrisy that he sees in Christians. This view is shared by many non-Christians, as evidenced in various polls which ask why people do not believe in Christianity. People outside of the Christian faith observe that we don't practice what we preach and conclude that church is a joke. They dislike us for being pious, holier-than-thou types whose lives are every bit as messy as everyone else's. We go to church on Sunday and then live Monday through Saturday as if our faith has nothing to do with how we are supposed to act. People perceive that we use our faith to support our own ideologies rather than allowing our faith to shape our words and actions.

Whether it's fudging a little on our tax returns or marital infidelity (recent studies show the rates for infidelity are no different between Christians and non-Christians), most of us don't display a level of morality that is very different from those who don't follow Jesus. When biblical principles intersect with real life, it's hard to make the difficult, practical, day-to-day decisions that tangibly show that we are called to a different standard. We wrestle with deep issues—anger, pride, and selfishness—that play out in sinful patterns in everyday life.

Another word that describes the state of many Christians today is *apathy*. Why is Christianity more and more in the margins of our culture? Perhaps people are apathetic about the church because the church is apathetic about the world. We have received the remarkable grace and forgiveness of God, but we seem to be hoarding it rather than passing it on. We invest so much into building our Christian subculture and taking care of ourselves that there is little left to invest in the world around us.

Jesus told us that His followers are the salt of the earth. But if we lose our saltiness, we will get thrown out and trampled underfoot. We no longer serve any purpose. Is that a picture of the church today?

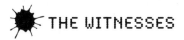 THE WITNESSES

The Bible calls Christians to a high standard. We are Christ's ambassadors, and as such, we are supposed to reflect the values and ideas that Jesus taught. Instead, we have often invoked Jesus' name to support our own agenda. We have claimed to be His followers but have lived lives that do not reflect Him. We have done a poor job of representing God. As a result, we have damaged the reputation of Christ and His church. There are many Christian public figures who display these shortcomings in very obvious ways. Let me share just a couple of recent examples, along with some ideas on how we could have done a better job reflecting the character of Jesus.

Jerry Falwell made a statement shortly after the terrorist attacks on 9/11. (In fairness to Falwell, he later apologized for his statement.) He placed "a lot of the blame [for the destructive hijackings]" on the federal courts "for throwing God out of the public square" and on those "who have tried to secularize America: pagans, abortionists, feminists, gays and lesbians who are actively trying to make that an alternative lifestyle, the ACLU, and People for the American Way." Unfortunately, this type of statement is quite typical of modern evangelical leaders. We Christians perceive ourselves to be modern-day prophets, showing outrage at the lack of morality that we see in the world around us. Unfortunately, as we stand and speak boldly we tend to forget our own faults and flaws, our own anger and pride. We rarely see the collapse that has occurred within the church itself.

Jesus taught that we should not pick at the speck in our neighbor's eye while we ignore the plank in our own eye. Before we can address the serious moral problems and decay in our culture, Christians need to address some of the issues that pervade Christian culture. It is much easier to speak out against evil in the world than to fix the evil in our own lives. Perhaps instead of proclaiming God's judgment on the world, we need to focus more on the church. In the Bible, God's judgment was most often on His chosen people, not on other people groups. A recent article in *Prism* magazine says, "All of us [Christians] deserve judgment, especially the church, for what the world has become."

Let me offer another example. Though some may not agree with me on this one, I think it is a compelling picture of how Christian culture has focused on morality as opposed to love. In the wake of the Monica Lewinsky scandal, Christians condemned Bill Clinton for his actions. The conservative Christian political machine bore down on the Clinton administration like a pack of wolves on a wounded animal. They saw their chance to gain political power through the president's behavior and cover-ups. I would never condone Bill Clinton's actions—his behavior was wrong. But should Christians use the weakness of this man to attempt to destroy him politically? In an interview with the *Washington Times* in 1997, Clinton was quoted as saying, "I've been in politics long enough to expect criticism and hostility. But I was unprepared for the hatred I get from Christians. Why do Christians hate so much?"

Clearly, the president lied and tried to justify behavior that was inappropriate. But I don't think that Jesus would have responded in the same way that most of us who call ourselves His followers did. I am reminded of the story in the gospel of John about the woman caught in adultery. The religious leaders of the day had caught this woman red-handed in sexual sin, and they were ready to kill her. According to their laws, they had every right to. But Jesus didn't back them up. He took this opportunity to speak directly and powerfully into this woman's life and change her heart (see 8:1-11). As far as Bill Clinton goes, I am honestly not sure what the proper response to this situation would be, but I do know that we didn't score any points in this battle. Perhaps Christians speaking into the life of the president with grace, love, and firm truth would have impacted his life in a tremendous way. Instead, our vicious response conveyed only anger and hatred. We are called to speak the truth in love, which means that we never condone sin, but that we confront people with grace and tact.

In addition to these specific incidents, examples of the wrongs done by other public figures or radical groups within the church are plentiful. Over and over we are confronted with outrageous acts performed in the name of Christianity. Whether it is the preacher on the corner who is screaming about the eternal damnation awaiting those who don't repent, or the televangelist promising health and wealth to those who send their donations, we see how the message of Christ is so often and easily distorted by those who profess to be His followers.

Examples like these show how the tone of our cultural dialogue has become one where Christians decry the collapse of morality in our society, while those outside of the church look at us and see no evidence of anything more redeeming in our Christian culture. We devolve into a war of words, pointing fingers and yelling, all the time widening the chasm between us and the world that we are called to engage and love, only reinforcing the notion that we are hypocrites.

TAKING THE STAND

Though people cite historical mistakes and high-profile figures as reasons for avoiding Christianity, I believe that at the core people are hurt most by those who are closest to them. So many individuals have been hurt by Christians in their lives, suffering at the hands of friends and family who are supposed to love them. I have encountered numerous people who have been badly damaged by their churches. Perhaps they grew up in legalistic, judgmental environments; they have seen how Christians behave and now, as adults, they want nothing to do with Christianity or the church. Their pain and hurt is real, but how do I explain that this is not what Jesus intended the church to be?

It is likely the way in which average Christians like me live our daily lives that does the most damage to the image of Christianity. While it is easy to point fingers and identify the flaws I see in other people, the reality is that my own shortcomings are just as destructive. And because my failures can be seen up-close and in person, the impact that they have on people around me is potentially far more severe. Until I own the fact that my own life has been every bit as off-putting as anyone else's, I will never be able to live and love as Jesus calls me to. I am just fortunate that my mistakes are not broadcast on national television. The truth is that if there were personal, individual examples of people who lived like Jesus, I believe people could get past the negative public examples.

The truth is that I am a prideful, hypocritical man. I am rarely compassionate. I can be cutting, back-biting, and hurtfully sarcastic. I insulate myself from the world and surround myself with people who think and believe just like I do. I project an attitude of having life all figured out, but I haven't got a clue most of the time! I want so much for my life to reflect Jesus, but it happens much too rarely.

I do have good intentions about living out my Christian faith. I want my love for Jesus to shine. I want to be able to give and serve sacrificially and to reflect the fruits of the Holy Spirit. But too often intention doesn't lead to action. I have been so conditioned by the attitudes and values of American culture that my life seems to reflect the pursuit of self-interest, comfort, and personal pleasure more than the pursuit of God. I am continually challenged to live radically as Jesus did, but the pull of work, family, friends, television, and all-around busyness prove too strong to allow me to escape the comfortable confines of my routine.

The message that my life sends is that being a follower of Jesus means that I engage in some religious activities once or twice a week, but it does not significantly change how I live. Jesus calls us to love our neighbors as we love ourselves, but most of the time I am too wrapped up in my own life to be able to invest in the lives of others. If I could love as Jesus did, it would send a completely different message. Instead of judging people who are different from me, I could reach out and seek real dialogue. Instead of being consumed by my own busyness, I could invest my time and energy into the lives of people around me. Instead of being caught in consumerism and debt, I could give generously to those with tremendous needs. Instead of tearing people down, I could continually seek to build others up. Instead of pride and competition, I could rejoice in the gifts and strengths and successes of others. How revolutionary this would be! How engaging and attractive to those who would observe Jesus at work in my life!

I'm sorry.

 WHY?

Clearly, in many ways, Christians (particularly myself) have missed the mark. We are going through the motions of church and ministry without ever really deeply encountering God. We talk about God, we know about God, but we rarely experience God. We can argue about creation and evolution, we can cite facts and invoke logic to prove the existence of God, but at the core, it is our personal experience of Christ's love, grace, and transforming power that will draw people to Jesus. We cannot communicate our experience with Christ if we have not really experienced Christ. We haven't yet fully immersed ourselves in God's love and haven't learned how to love like Him.

E. Stanley Jones, missionary to India in the early twentieth century, talked of the importance of communicating our experience with Christ. As missionaries brought the gospel to India, they found that people wanted Christ without all of the trappings and baggage of the Western church. In the same way today, people are drawn to Jesus, but they don't want all of the religious baggage that has come to be associated with Christianity. As we separate Jesus from the behaviors of the church, we can recover what it really means to be a Christian. We are not watering down the message, we are returning to the core, the truth of the message, which is Jesus!

A NEW (OLD) VISION

Because I love the church and still believe that God has called us to be salt and light in this world, I am willing to break out of those habits and patterns and traditions that I find so comfortable and seek to change in order to become the church that Jesus calls us to be. The model that I can use is the first century church described in the Scriptures. I've often read the stories of the early church and wondered why they were able to impact their communities and the world so deeply, while our lives and our Christian communities don't seem to have the same power. When I read about the early church, I see a few key differences between the church as it existed two thousand years ago and the church today:

1. Community. The first century church was defined by close-knit community. Christians cared for each other, putting the needs of others before their own. They supported and encouraged one another in real ways.
2. Respect of outsiders. Christians were respected by non-believers. When people became followers of Christ, their lives showed real transformation, and people saw and respected their honesty and work ethic.
3. Transformation of culture. The local church in each city impacted its community. It brought new ideas, culture, and values to the world and made a deep and lasting impact.

So if this is how the church is supposed to be, how did we get to where we are today? Why does there seem to be so little genuine community in the church? Why is there such a lack of respect for the church from outsiders? And, most importantly, why does the church no longer have a transforming impact on culture? The simple answer is that we have drifted away from the basic things that are supposed to define us: love and holiness. As followers of Christ, we are supposed to reflect God's character in our lives through the power of the Holy Spirit in us. What does that mean? The God that we serve is a God of perfect love. His love for us is unconditional and boundless. But He is also a God of perfect holiness, who cannot tolerate sin. As people who have committed our lives to following Him, we are called to exhibit these characteristics to the world around us. It is only then that we begin to become the people that God intended us to be.

If we go back and look at the early church, we see how these qualities of love and holiness manifested themselves and fostered the community, respect, and transformation that allowed the church to grow and thrive. Community is born out of true love for God and for other believers. As we genuinely love one another, we move past politeness and shallow relationships into true community, where we share in each other's life, where we are able to encourage and challenge one another in meaningful ways. Respect from others is gained as Christians exhibit a standard of holiness without moral compromise. And transformation of our culture occurs when love and holiness combine in a group of people who love God passionately and are committed to impacting the world around them.

Our challenge is learning how to exhibit both love and holiness working together. As Christians, we cannot and should not condone or tolerate sin. Right is right and wrong is wrong. But to pass judgment on individuals without love is not a true expression of God's holiness. We need to change our approach. As Paul says in Ephesians 4:15, we are to be "speaking the truth in love." We need people who will boldly stand against evil in the world. But we need people who will speak out in a way that shows genuine love and care for the people we are addressing. It is so easy to stand against something, to condemn someone. It is much more difficult to provide positive alternatives, or to come alongside an individual who is struggling and tell him, "I will love you and support you in every way that I possibly can." Christians speak of how we must hate the sin, but love the sinner. This is message that Jesus preached. Sadly, though we repeat these words to ourselves, our lives rarely reflect that kind of attitude. What we say with our lives is "hate the sin, humiliate and reject the sinner."

We earlier defined the problem in the church as hypocrisy and apathy. Love and holiness are the antithesis of hypocrisy and apathy. Hypocrisy stems from a lifestyle that compromises holiness. Apathy comes from lack of love for God and each other. If we can begin to live out the love and holiness of God, we will find that hypocrisy and apathy slowly disappear from our experience.

 ## MAKING THE CHANGE

How do we begin to change? It's difficult. We will never fully succeed until we reach heaven. But I am encouraged by what appears to be a new movement beginning in the church. People are beginning to recognize that some of the ways that we have done things in the past are not working.

In Mark 7:13, Jesus chastises religious leaders, telling them that they are "invalidating the word of God by [their] tradition" (NASB). It is so easy to get caught up in the way that we have always done things that we lose sight of God's word and His intent for the church. Sometimes the most Christian thing we can do is to break away from the status quo. Just because we have always done things this way doesn't mean it's right. Christianity, when we are doing it right, is going to be messy. We are going to be uncomfortable. We are going to have to embrace some people that we don't like. We may even have to deal with stains on the carpets.

Loving our neighbors means taking a long look at our own lives and examining those things that potentially push them away. John Fischer wrote an excellent book called *Twelve Steps for the Recovering Pharisee (like me)*. Many of us fall into that category, having forsaken love and grace for rules and regulations. Recovering Pharisees realize that they are not perfect people with all of the answers but simple individuals who are immensely grateful for the grace and love of Jesus. It is easy to point fingers at the faults of other people, but as recovering Pharisees, we realize that we can only change ourselves.

We start by understanding that we must experience Jesus in a fresh way. We must drink deeply of His love so that we can reflect His grace and goodness to the world around us. I pray for the strength and wisdom for myself and each one of us to learn to follow the footsteps of Jesus. I pray that we would encounter Jesus in ways that are so real and powerful that we cannot help but become like Him.

We progress when we realize that many of the things we invest time and energy into are not really the things people need. The things we have defined as important are not really what Jesus calls us to focus on. We spend a lot of time on events and services, instead of building community and caring for the needs of people around us. We need to step out of that comfortable routine that doesn't demand too much of us, and move past a church culture that allows us to attend entertaining (and occasionally challenging) services every week but does not compel us to invest much of ourselves outside of that.

The church can be a place where people are embraced. It can be a group of people who have discovered the amazing grace of our God and are striving together to become more like Him. The church is to be a place where we struggle and grow together and are free to be honest, open, and real with one another as we seek to grow in our love for Christ.

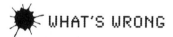 WHAT'S WRONG

The bottom line is that Christians have come up short of what Jesus calls us to be. The result is that in America in the early twenty-first century, Christianity has developed a bad reputation. We have much to apologize for. We recognize that the church will never be perfect. It is made up of flawed people who will sometimes make poor decisions. But we need to do a better job of owning our mistakes and striving to be the people that we are called to be. In my life, I haven't done that. The story of my life is the story of a man who has been hypocritical and judgmental, a man who has struggled and strived to lead a life that is worthy of the name Christian, but has often fallen short. And I fear that my shortcomings have contributed to the perceptions that so many have about the church.

But I love Jesus, and I love the church enough to want to change. I want my life to be a reflection of Jesus' character. I want our churches to point people to Jesus.

On one occasion, the *London Times* posed a question to several writers, including G. K. Chesterton, a popular British journalist and outspoken Christian in the early twentieth century, asking them, "What is wrong with the world?" Chesterton's response was the briefest and probably the most poignant. His response was simply, "I am."

So I owe a debt to Chesterton as I ask myself the question, "What is wrong with the church?" I find that the most honest answer I can give is "I am."

I'm sorry.

STEVE CONRAD is the missional director at the Upper Room community in Minneapolis, MN (www.upperroomcommunity.org). He is also a musician.

DETOXING FROM CHURCH

JASON ZAHARIADES / OCTOBER 1, 2003

BEGINNING THE PROCESS

Back in February, as Mark Feliciano and I were praying and talking about beginning a missional community, I emailed a guy on the other side of the U.S. who had already begun one of these communities. Here are a couple of things he said in our correspondences:

> Here's a strong statement: Most evangelicals, including Vineyard people, are addicted to church culture. Take away their Sunday service, their Bible studies, prayer meetings, and five-song worship teams, and they start having withdrawals quickly. I think that it is a necessary part of this process to have a detox time. . . . I would suggest a time of at least a year of not doing the "normal" church stuff. For us, during that time of detachment we only did a few things together: ask hard questions and eat. Those were our corporate disciplines.

In another email he reinforced the point:

> Let me reiterate from my last email that one of the most beneficial things you might do is take a break from all things church for a while. This may seem really counterproductive, especially when you start having people wanting to be a part of your community immediately. But if your aim is to get people to begin

thinking outside the bounds of cultural Christianity, some significantly radical action is required.

When I first read these comments, I knew he was stating something profound. What I didn't anticipate was the extent of my own addiction to the contemporary church and the painful detox process I would experience. What I'm coming face to face with through the process is the inauthenticity and impotence of my own faith. Let me explain.

MY ADDICTION TO "CHURCH"

In the Americanized church, the organization is designed to turn life and faith into a simple prepackaged consumer product. This is what John Drane calls the "McDonaldization of the Church."

I need to worship. So I go to my local church, which, if it's cutting-edge, has a worship pastor on staff that prepares an inspiring "worship experience" for me on a weekly basis. One local church I know advertises its worship services on its marquee, "We worship five times, three ways, one God." (Hello! Is it me, or does that just sound wrong?)

I need to fellowship with my fellow Christians. So I go to my local church to attend a programmed version of community that provides a surface-level contact with people around some form of activity at my convenience. If I need more fellowship, I go to a small group, usually focused on the dynamic personality of the small group leader or on the subject matter I feel I need to better my life. But again, this is at my convenience and fairly optional if my schedule becomes too demanding.

I need discipleship and Christian growth. So I go to my local church to attend Sunday services, Bible studies, and small groups where someone opens the Bible and tells me what it says and how it should apply to my life. I also have the option of learning "practical" topics such as how to be a good spouse, parent, employee, leader, steward, etc.

I need to serve. So I go to my local church and participate in a program where I use my time and skills in a fairly convenient manner to help others. For the most part, it's fairly safe. And if I'm a volunteer, my participation is completely based on my schedule.

I need to be engaged in mission. So I go to my local church to connect to their evangelistic ministry and their missions program. Every so often I might volunteer to hand out sodas or serve coffee in a convenient and semirelational form of "reaching people" for Christ. I might also give money to local missionaries the church supports and maybe participate in a weekend mission trip.

I need a children's program to educate my kids. So I go to my local church to place my children in the care of Sunday school teachers and youth pastors who will provide the spiritual and moral foundation for their Christian growth via an age-relevant program.

I need purpose for my life. So I go to my local church, hoping to find a leader with a vision big enough to inspire me. Then I sacrifice my time, energy, and money to become involved in the leader's vision so I can build something big for God with him. New programs. New buildings. New projects. New groups. New services. New converts. New church plants. New missions. More and more and more vision to give my life a reason to exist.

To make matters worse, as a pastor on staff, all of my relationships and ministries are mediated through my title and position in the organization. An unhealthy symbiotic relationship occurs between me and the organization as my life and faith becomes synonymous with the success of the organization. If we, as leaders, can design an organization that satisfies the consumer needs of a couple hundred people, well, then we must be doing something right in God's kingdom. And the more people we reach, then the better we are. So I preach, lead worship, administrate, counsel, teach, organize, recruit, train, write, and do practically everything as a "pastor" of an organization. Eventually my identity becomes distorted by what I do for the church. What's worse, my role and effectiveness as a staff pastor are intimately connected to my own formation and personal development. This continues to blur the line between my personal life and faith and my abilities as a leader of an organization.

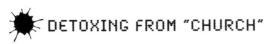 DETOXING FROM "CHURCH"

Now strip all of that away. Imagine what you would have left after you remove from your life everything connected with the organizational church. I mean everything. I've discovered the hard way that living most of my adult life in cultural Christianity has formed my entire identity as a Christian. And when everything in my life connected with the church is gone, including sixteen years of professional ministry, I'm confronted with the true raw status of my personal faith.

Now I'm going to say something harsh: In order to *be* the Church, we need to leave the church. In other words, in order to truly become God's people as He intended, we must abandon our cultural version of organizational church. The application of this statement might vary, but it must happen. And as we abandon the church to become the Church, we will go through a detox period.

Why such drastic measures? Involvement in an organizational, consumer-driven church blinds us to the real state of our lives. By participating in this kind of church I can enjoy inspiring worship, biblical exposition of Scripture, fellowship, small groups, kids' programs, service projects, missions, discipleship, books, radio broadcasts, multimedia presentations, and virtually anything else I need in my spiritual life. In fact, I can enjoy an entirely alternative lifestyle where Christianity is prepackaged for me — books, music, entertainment, news reports, advice, etc. And as I consume it, it forms a facade over the real condition of my life. The rub is when my true condition actually bubbles to the surface and I find myself troubled, discontent, or miserable. Then the church or the pastor or the worship team has lost the "anointing," and I must find a new organizational church that will provide me with what I need to feel better about who I am.

In this distorted perspective, I fail to recognize that the true state of my life and faith is who I am and what I do in relation to God and His kingdom, not who I am and what I do in relation to the church.

MOVING FROM BEING CHURCHED TO BEING THE CHURCH

Detoxing from any kind of substance abuse is only a means to a much greater end. It is the essential process toward a healthy life, free from oppressive addiction. The same is true for one who detoxes from the church. Remember, we must leave the church in order to *be* the Church. We must stop being churched and start being the Church.

What is the Church? It is a community of people who are each following Christ into His divine life and love here on earth. People who are learning how to become by grace what Christ is by nature—the full and complete emptying of self in order to participate fully in God's kingdom so as to be a redemptive force that recreates all aspects of life and creation (see Romans 8:19-21; Philippians 2:5-16; Colossians 1:19-20). The Church is a group of Christ followers who are sent as Jesus was sent (see John 20:21). In this way, the Church is the continuation of Christ's incarnation on earth.

These and other biblical aspects of the Church run counter to cultural Christianity and its addictive, prepackaged, consumerist version of the church. Being the Church is about who I am and who I am becoming as I follow Christ individually and in a community. Being the Church is becoming like Christ so together, I and other Christ followers may continue His incarnation in and to the world.

A primary difference between being churched and being the Church is how I approach the community. Being churched assumes the organizational church is designed from the perspective that I am a consumer of religious goods and service. Therefore, I am expected to participate in the church's programs chiefly to receive and consume. It's the organization's responsibility to program, coordinate, and provide what I need for my spiritual satisfaction.

But being the Church requires me to take full responsibility to follow Christ and Christ alone into His life. I can't say this enough: We are to become by grace what Jesus is by nature. And He did not have an organization mediating His life and faith. He had a relationship with the Father by walking in the Spirit, expressed through a life of spiritual disciplines. Then He invites us to learn from Him how to develop the same kind of intimate relationship with the Father in the same way (see Matthew 11:27-30).

The Christian community is then made up of Christ followers who encourage, challenge, pray, minister, learn, honor, love, and spur each other on. But it is not the community's nor the community leaders' responsibility to program or lead others into divine life. Only Christ can do that. So while my needs remain the same, I must look not to an organization, but to Christ alone to lead me into His divine life and love.

I still need to worship. But I am to worship first as an individual follower of Christ daily. I am a priest, offering all of my life back to God in constant prayer, joy, and thankfulness (see 1 Thessalonians 5:16-18). Then, from the overflow of my personal worship, I join in corporate worship with others who also worship God on a daily basis.

I still need to fellowship. But now I must actually alter my schedule and hang out with people in real ways: over meals, over coffee, at my home or theirs. This also means that there isn't a program or an event to generate fellowship. I have to initiate. I have to be prepared to discuss life and faith in real ways that encourage and build up. I have to be prepared to be used by Christ to pray, listen, minister, laugh, cry, confront, encourage, and so on, all on the leading of the Spirit and not at the cue of a leader or scheduled time in a service.

I still need discipleship and growth. But now I must walk with Christ, by grace in the Spirit through a life of spiritual discipline. I must follow

Christ into a curriculum of spiritual disciplines that transforms my inner world into Christ's inner life. As such, I must study the Bible. I must pray. I must meditate. I must take my own personal retreats. I must read. I must educate myself. I must become theologically astute and spiritually vibrant. I must discover God's will for my life and not some canned version from a pastor who talks at me for forty-five minutes each week. I must put the same or more energy and time into my personal faith than I do into my occupation, education, and entertainment.

I still need to serve. But now I must look for the opportunities in my life. I can't enjoy the safety of a program with other Christians. I must view my entire life as service to the people I live with and live around. I must discover the poor and marginalized in my life and be Christ to them. I can't just give money to the organization to do it for me.

I still need to engage in mission. But now I must actually *be* a witness of Christ's eternal divine life to the people I live with, work with, play with, and shop with. I must actually be a living, albeit flawed, example of divine life on earth. I must be able to say, "When you see me, you see the Father." Then I must view my family, my neighborhood, my job, and my entire life as my mission field. Not in the imperialistic way the church has done evangelism and missions, but in the winsome, educated, and Spirit-led way that drew thousands to Jesus when He walked this earth.

I still need to raise my children in life and faith. But now I carry the lion's share of the responsibility. As their parent, my faith and life form their faith and life. I must learn to dialogue at their level. I must lead them in prayer, in worship, in fellowship, in spiritual disciplines, in service, in mission, in play.

I still need purpose for my life. But now I learn from Christ how to be like Him so I can live like Him—completely toward God for the sake of the world.

THE PROPER ROLE OF COMMUNITY

Now I know, having read everything so far, it is easy to conclude, "Then I don't need community." That couldn't be further from the truth. What we don't need is the organizational consumer church as a provider of religious goods and services. The consumer ethic of our surrounding culture has infected the organizational church turning pastors into entrepreneurs and CEOs and turning Christians into consumers.

Once we understand what it means to be the people of God and to shoulder the personal responsibility of transformation into Christlikeness, then we begin to realize we need authentic Christian community more than ever. Let me explain.

In *Renovation of the Heart*, Dallas Willard lays out a general pattern for personal transformation. He states: "If we are to be spiritually formed in Christ, we must have and must implement the appropriate *vision*, *intention*, and *means* [VIM]. . . . If this VIM pattern is not put in place properly and held there, Christ simply will not be formed in us."[1] This pattern for spiritual formation is a fine balance between the individual and the community. First, the vision essential for transformation is a vision of life now and forever in God's will, partaking in the divine nature (see 2 Peter 1:4) and participating by our actions in what God is doing now in our lifetime on earth.[2] This vision is given to humanity by God, revealed to God's covenant people, the Jews, and given fullest expression in Jesus. As such, a personal vision for life in the kingdom comes directly from the living Christ, but is also mediated through God's covenant community, the Church.

Second, the intention for spiritual formation is brought to completion only by a decision to fulfill or carry through with the intention. In this case, the intention to obey the model and teachings of Jesus must be "sealed" with an individual's decision to actually obey Christ in all of life. The intention and decision, which lie in the realm and responsibility of the individual, can only be formed and sustained by a forceful vision, which comes directly from Christ and is supplemented by the community.

Willard makes a significant point in this area:

> Our beliefs and feelings cannot be changed by a choice. We
> cannot just choose to have different beliefs or feelings. But we
> do have some liberty to take in different ideas and information
> and to think about things in different ways. We can choose to
> take in the Word of God, and when we do that, beliefs and feel-
> ings will be steadily pulled in a godly direction.[3]

In other words, the will is moved by insight into truth and reality, which,
in turn, evoke emotion appropriate to a new state of the will. This is how
real inward change occurs. The consumer-based church does the exact
opposite, trying to motivate and inspire people to choose to believe and
do things they really don't believe. This approach does not result in any
lasting spiritual formation.

Finally, the vision and intention to follow and obey Christ will naturally
lead to seeking out and applying the means to that end. Scripture and
church history are replete with the appropriate means for spiritual formation. The key is to target the aspects of our humanity—the thoughts,
feelings, will, social relations, and bodily inclinations—with the abundant individual and corporate spiritual disciplines available to us so that
we become people who naturally and easily embody Christlikeness.[4] In
this way, the statement "Where there is a will, there is a way" rings true
for spiritual formation.

To illustrate this process, Willard makes an interesting statement, "Any
successful plan for spiritual formation, whether for the individual or
group, will in fact be significantly similar to the Alcoholics Anonymous
program."[5] In AA, the participant envisions the potential new life of
sobriety and freedom from addiction that is available to him or her. The
vision is then pursued with an intention to realize it, actuated by a decision. The means are then applied to produce the desirable state.

The program illustrates the important balance between the individual and
the community. The individual must possess the vision, supplemented by

the relational structure of the AA group. The intention and its accompanying decision rest solely on the individual. The means are then carried out primarily by the individual throughout his or her daily life, supported by the relationships and structure of the local AA community. The point is that as important as the community is, success and failure of AA in an individual's life rests primarily on the individual's intention to follow through daily. The community exists to support the individual's pursuit of sobriety.

The Christian community's role is very similar. Willard states that God's plan for spiritual formation through the local Christian community is threefold: First, create an ethos and culture that has as its center apprenticeship to Christ in all the minute aspects of life. This creates the necessary vision to fuel the individual's intention. Second, immerse apprentices at all levels of growth in the Trinitarian presence of God through the community's structure and life. In this way, the community's primary purpose is to encounter the Trinitarian presence and hold people up within it. Finally, arrange for the inner transformation of people in such a way that doing the words and deeds of Christ is not the focus but the natural outcome or side effect.[6]

This creates a community of Christ's apprentices, in which each member is pursuing Christ, spending time with Him in the course of his or her daily life in order to learn how to be like Him. When the community gathers, all relationships are then mediated through Christ. Willard describes this Christocentric community in *The Divine Conspiracy*:

> In the spiritual community there is never any immediate relationship between human beings. Another way of saying this is that among those who live as Jesus' apprentices, there are no relationships that omit the presence and action of Jesus. We never go "one on one"; all relationships are mediated through him. I never think simply of what I am going to do with you, to you, or for you. I think of what we, Jesus and I, are going to do with you, to you, and for you. Likewise, I never think of what you

are going to do with me, to me, and for me, but of what will be done by you and Jesus with me, to me, and for me.[7]

In this way, Christ fills all of our needs for life and formation as we follow Him (see 2 Peter 1:3) not as we participate in and consume the organizational church's programs. As I follow the resurrected Christ with others who are following Him, He meets us and ministers to us through all the members of the community.

 CONCLUSION

As our understanding of being the Church changes, the role of proper Christian community changes. We discover a deeper need for authentic community than any of us realized existed. As a follower of Christ, I constantly need my fellow Christ followers. I cannot enter into Christ's divine life and love apart from Christ-mediated community with them. His life and love are expressed in fully giving myself to them (see Ephesians 5:1-2). Therefore, I need to be with my fellow Christ followers so I can serve them, love them, and pour out on them everything I am becoming in Christ for their benefit. And they need to do that for me. Together, fully giving ourselves to each other, we continue on into Christlikeness.

This kind of Christian community is essential to grow into Christ's life. Christ is formed in each of His apprentices as they engage His abundant grace in daily living through a life of spiritual disciplines. As each Christ follower shoulders his or her responsibility of following Jesus into the life He has mastered and alone can share, all are then supported by Christ as each member brings Christ being formed in them to the community.

Only Christ is the source of divine life. Each member must follow Jesus daily to learn His divine life. Each member must shoulder the responsibility to work out his or her salvation and not expect the community or its leaders to do it for him or her. In Christ, we can learn together, serve together, grow together, love together, and so on. But we must first and foremost follow Christ into His life. And to do this we must abandon the distorted and addictive version of the consumer church in order to be free to become Christ's Church.

JASON ZAHARIADES is married to an incredible woman and has four great kids. He enjoys dates with his wife, watching good movies, reading good theology books, and tinkering with writing. Jason has an MA in theology from Fuller Theological Seminary. He currently coleads a small house church (www.theofframp.org) as well as attends a local church. He enjoys helping people in all church environments to become better apprentices of Jesus so that together we may implement God's new creation in this world.

CHANGING TO STAY THE SAME

RYAN MELLING / JANUARY 16, 2004

 GRASSROOTS

Grassroots is not such a popular term in the organizational church today. It seems to suggest an overwhelming power given to the people. It seems to suggest that there may not be such a heavy need for paid professionals. It certainly suggests less need for multifunctional building. It is an idea that does put power into the hands of the people. Instead of the few leading the masses, perhaps we would find full participants in the function of God's people in this world.

What an exciting challenge for us in leadership. It seems to challenge our very motives for being involved in ministry. To empower people to take leadership is to create an even more powerful movement. It gives ownership to all who desire it. Unfortunately, it seems like it could work us right out of a job. But perhaps this is not such a bad thing. When we look at the lives of the early believers, we do not see them defining their calling as the group of people willing to offer the most secure and comfortable life. In fact, their calling was a dangerous adventure. If we move in this direction, perhaps we will remember what it means to pick up our cross and follow Christ.

This does not sit well with pastors in any denomination. Quite frankly, it does not sit so well with me. It is a little scary not to have that security. Not to know where your next paycheck will come from. To be fully dependant on God, who we know to be our Creator and our Sustainer. We know that He feeds the birds, and we know He clothes the flowers. It is another thing to trust your life to that reality.

In a grassroots, or what I will call "organic," structure, we are free to move, free to change, free to create, and free to empower anyone, anywhere, anytime. When Philip saw the Ethiopian on the road in Acts 8, he did not invite him to go through step-by-step classes at his church to become a disciple of Christ; instead, Philip offered the opportunity right there on the spot (see verses 26-40). Can we truly understand the absolute power in this? We seem to think that we must know people inside and out and, further, make sure their theology is completely accurate (at least according to our own) before we would give someone that right. Yet Philip did it right there and then, seemingly after an acquaintance of mere minutes. Even more, Philip was quickly gone. He was not around to keep this person in check or make sure he stayed theologically straight.

This kind of empowerment tends to scare us. It certainly scares me. It seems sloppy. It seems careless. But perhaps we can look at it in a different light. What it may be is God's free gift, to completely enter into His world, into His kingdom. Through the union between Christ and us, this is fully possible. We must really take confidence in Jesus' words that whoever seeks will find. We must be assured in the promise that God will continue His good work in us.

When we can take this organic stance towards the church, amazing power comes just through our ability to be completely flexible to God's plan. We once again rely on God to speak to us while we journey through this life with Him close by our side. Jesus said that wherever two or more are gathered in His name, He will be there. Isn't this also church? Isn't it wherever the Spirit of God is? So then, doesn't it happen far more often than once or even twice per week? We cannot go to church because we are the church. We do not attend a church because we live and breathe it. This is what distinguishes us from the rest of the world.

 CREATORS OF CULTURE

To think of activism in any form is to think of change. Any movement is ultimately concerned with it. Movements form as people gather around similar visions for change and move society toward those visions.

As the church, our vision is the kingdom of God. It must be clear that this is not a vision that we can fully realize in this life. Of course, we are sinful people, and this continually guides us off track on our journey in this kingdom. However, this does not give us any excuse to settle. We cannot look at what we've created as the church today and claim, "This is it. There is no more we can do as a sinful people."

Henry David Thoreau said, in his essay "Civil Disobedience," that even America and democracy should not be seen as the end in our governmental evolution. Surely as the world has transformed in many ways from tribes and monarchies to socialism and dictatorship, democracy cannot be the absolute perfect manifestation of government. Certainly many of us who are disenfranchised with U.S. politics and policy dare to dream of a better way. We see the founding fathers as those who were tired of their old oppressive government and dared to dream of a better way. It created the most powerful culture the world has ever seen. But even they saw it only as a step in the evolution of government. Could there be even better?

The same is true in the civil rights movement. A large part of the American population dared to dream of a society that was concerned more with the character of a person than with the color of his skin. They dreamed of a society that would be free of racism and prejudice. Certainly we have come a long way, but even in this issue we must know we still have a long way to go.

Or what about our treatment of women and homosexuals or our attitudes toward the physically or mentally handicapped? Our society has become one of incredible accessibility and mobility for these groups of people as well, but certainly there is much further yet to go.

The Bible, from Old Testament to New, is full of examples of movement from one behavior to another and from one thought to another. In some cases it is radical change (repentance). In others it is simply a next step in a continuous movement of God. Deuteronomy 21 gives instructions on the "spoils of war" (verses 10-14). Reading this from our culture, we are appalled that God would tell His people that when they conquer a city they are permitted to take any woman as a wife, purely on desire. We cannot believe God would allow people to be treated in such a way. Yet to Deuteronomy's first readers, this directive is a giant leap forward. In this early culture, a soldier in a conquering army would have the right to have his way with any woman he desired, to use her as a sex slave, and then sell her when he tired of her. God brings His people a step forward in this passage. He tells His people that the women should be allowed to shave their heads and have a period of mourning. Then the soldier was to marry that woman and treat her as his wife. If he then decided to leave her, she was not to be sold as a slave. This was incredible news for the original hearers of this message.

As time passes, God's people continue to change. However, as we see with Jesus' many confrontations with the Pharisees, it is not always for the best. At times we must promote a change of the heart (repenting to deal with sin that has led us off course). We find ourselves, as church leaders, in quite the same predicament that the Pharisees of Jesus' time found themselves in. They were largely concerned with the outside deeds of the people and the keeping of the law. Brian McLaren describes their evolution in theology quite well in his book *Adventures in Missing the Point*. In it he demonstrated that the people of God had always been saved from their oppressors. From Moses to David, God always sent a savior in His people's time of need. The Jews around the time of Jesus had been in this state of oppression for quite some time, and people began to wonder why there was no savior. The Pharisees were a group of people who had come to the conclusion that it was because of the people's sin that the Messiah was not coming. So every law was meticulously carried out, but only for the sake of the law itself.

Our actions tend to give us away. As leaders we surely say that one can only be saved by grace and through faith. We believe this in our minds, and we speak it from our mouths, but in practice we tell ourselves and each other who the real Christians are, and we define them by their actions. James declares that faith without deeds is dead. This is true, but surely deeds without faith are completely meaningless. I am certain that there are many who wear the deeds of Christianity without ever having known the grace of our Lord and really put their faith in His saving power. Isn't this more dangerous than a deedless faith? Isn't that exactly what Jesus condemned the Pharisees for, action with no heart?

When Jesus came, He called His people to an entirely different change: a change of the heart and of our innermost being. To move us forward by starting at the core of who we are. This is the brilliance of Jesus. To recognize that it is the heart that controls all action. Without that initial change, there is no point in changing any other behavior. Jesus was creating an entirely new culture, and He was instilling it into the heart of His followers. Perhaps we must continually regain that heart as we move forward in this movement.

And move forward we must. The world continues to change. Today it is changing faster than ever before and there is no sign of slowing down. Scholars define the last five hundred years (roughly) as the modern era. Today they are seeing an entire culture shift that is being dubbed postmodern. Where the modern era was filled with science and imperialism, the postmodern world is filled with far more relative truth and an appreciation for what is unknown. Where modern theology was filled with proofs and laws, these no longer offer relief in the searching postmodern world. We are on the cusp of a very defining time (and perhaps even this postmodern era will change to a post-postmodern era within our lifetime). It is with that in mind that we must continue to move forward together. To lead the world through these changes rather than attempting to pull the world back from them.

The church will continue to marginalize itself if it continues to hold fast to modern practice and theology. We must embrace this changing world, develop new language, find new metaphors. We should not take a position of fear in this change; in fact, we should be leading it. The world is in desperate need of our leadership. In the postmodern world relativism is king and knowledge is directly linked to experience. In new generations, where it is not uncommon to be a second or third generation removed from the church (that is to say that they have never experienced church on any level and neither have their parents or possibly grandparents) there is a widespread search for spirituality. Statistics show that spiritual interest is up and the search for something of significance is rising, but it is not Christianity that is meeting that interest, although it is not Christ these seekers are opposed to.

Perhaps our messages are conflicting. The church is what we invite people to join. It is not the life we live as Jesus intended it. So many have communicated frustration in feeling like the church is made up of people who fake their faith, living one way and behaving another when the right people are watching. Meaningless deeds.

I am always interested to see how pastors and priests are portrayed on television shows. In one episode of a new program, a mother walked by a minister (we knew this because of the collar) and, in her frustration with her family crisis, she asked something to the effect of "Why does God allow bad things to happen to good people?" To which the minister looked puzzled and proceeded to stumble over an answer that boiled down to "I'll pray for you." To which the mother responded, "What will you say to God when you pray for me?" The minister answered, "Help that frustrated lady in the parking lot?"

This is how much of the western world views us as Christians. This is one key signal that we are becoming less of a presence in our world. Most people think that we are all about rules and regulations. They are convinced that to become a Christian is to give up on ever having fun. There is no power behind our message anymore. I've had many friends who have told me they have never met a Christian like me. One of my friends told me he did not know that someone like me existed in the world. I don't say this to blow my own horn or prove to anyone how wonderful I am, but these are people who are not Christians. Many are past Christians, or at least had some contact with a church. One friend is the son of a pastor, and others are homosexuals who were kicked out of their churches. I had the chance to ask them what they meant by their comments, and it was something hard for them to put a finger on, but the best they could describe it was that I actually seemed to care about them and that it was obvious that I truly lived differently.

To my knowledge, these friends are still not Christians today. I, at least, did not lead them in any type of "Sinner's Prayer." I did not make sure that they knew they would be in heaven when they died. I did show them Christ, however. I did show them a drastically different picture of what Christianity is all about, and a door to Jesus was reopened as a result of our relationship.

This is our fight in the changing world: to, at the very least, keep up with it, but, even more, to lead it through the changes. Todd Hunter describes his years of church planting and how it has changed in terms of the questions asked. He says that when he began, the biggest question was whether you could play a guitar in church. Today that is a nonissue. People now ask what church is, what its function should be, and how do we live it out.

One of our key roles as the church is to create the culture of the kingdom of God as well as we can, and to invite the rest of the world into that experience with the Creator God. As a movement of God, we are creating a world where God is king, and through Jesus' sacrifice, we are united with Him and with each other. We must share this experience with the entire world. In order to communicate to this world, however, we must enter into serious questioning. Everything is up for grabs. Every idea and practice is suspect. Hopefully we will arrive at many similar conclusions, but if we are not allowed to ask the questions, we will find ourselves with meaningless actions and no heart to back it up. Questions are good. They are there to refine us and our way of thinking. Through the questions, we can enter into a world where we are constantly transformed through the renewing of our minds (see Romans 12:2).

There is tremendous power in the organic. God's power shows up in the natural course of life, and we must hold to our structures loosely in order to continue to allow the Holy Spirit to guide us. We cannot simply apply candles and PowerPoint to our church services and assume God will now meet a new people. We must be in authentic relationship with God and our communities for our own natural flares to come out in creating structures. Any structure we create will be corrupt, however. This is why it must be one that can continually be questioned so it can continue to change so we can continue to be the same force in the world.

I have considered my life to be one that is wrapped up in ministry and worship. Neither can be separated from my life. Through my life I have encountered many people who have been burned by the church in some way. I relate to them on that level, but what we do not share in common is our desire to continue our relationship with Christ and His kingdom. Through these relationships, my theology and orientation toward Christ has drastically changed. That is to say that I have come to understand God's movement in this world in a whole new way, and through the help of others I share ministry with, we have attempted to create a different church that is completely committed to God's kingdom on earth and bringing in the hurting and burned out people He is calling to Himself. We live our lives to this purpose, and new structures and metaphors have emerged to make sense of this journey. The above is an excerpt from a larger work being compiled that tells of this journey.

STRIPPING AWAY SECRET IDENTITIES

Why Your Church Isn't a Superhero

SARAH RAYMOND CUNNINGHAM / APRIL 27, 2007

The church is the hope of the world.

Or so I've been told time after time by well-meaning speakers looking to inspire me to go all out for Christ's mission.

And this kind of pep talk makes sense on the surface. After all, there are so many "lost" people who need "saving," the church would probably get onto rescuing more of them if we thought we were their only hope.

The only problem with donning our capes, emblazed with a capital *C*, of course, is that . . . well, let's just say there's a whole lot of kryptonite in the world. A whole lot of potential for failure.

And, just like the cartoon superheroes, we humans sometimes wander into a sinister trap without even noticing. In fact, what's worse is that we sometimes unknowingly set the trap for ourselves.

We set our hopes high, expecting the church to be the perfect mix of thought-provoking and warm-and-fuzzy, and then we are disappointed when the church doesn't appear to deliver. When the church gets caught up in pride over a big attendance spurt, when gossip is on the fast track through the church lobby, when the associate pastor runs off with the gorgeous young organist; we're left with our jaws hanging open. Our worldview, which rests on the church being the hope of the world, is dangerously close to meltdown.

Even scarier, now that some mammoth failure has pried our eyes open, we begin noticing flaw after flaw in the way our church is organized. And before long, our dissatisfaction turns to cynicism and our cynicism to jadedness.

So why, with our X-ray spiritual vision and tingling Holy Spirit sense, do we regularly walk right into disillusionment's evil dungeon? Sometimes disillusionment grabs hold of us because of something as simple as unrealistic expectations, such as these:

The church will always appreciate my investment. False. The tough reality is that other members of your church may not always notice or acknowledge when you've volunteered at four consecutive events or for four consecutive years, for that matter. They may not stuff your mailbox with thank-you cards or flowers, put your picture on the big screen, or burst into a mid-service standing ovation to thank you for how you've invested hours so their experience could be better.

The church will always take the time to understand me. Nope. In a church of flawed humans, there will be some people who will superficially gloss over you without ever nurturing a genuine relationship. Sadly, there will be some people who judge you based on insignificant criteria (like what you wear) and who won't take the time to listen to truly understand your concerns.

The church will always offer the kind of support I need when I need it. Myth! Sometimes when you encounter a difficult life stage, the people in your church may fail to notice you could use some extra encouragement. Unfortunately, they may not even realize you've missed services for a while. And, even worse, there are some among them who may gossip about your situation rather than help you heal.

The church leadership is 100 percent admirable. Wrong answer! The church leaders, although more studied and sometimes (but not always) more seasoned in the faith, have plenty of potential for failure. They have their own personality flaws, their own weaknesses, and their own temptations. And like attendees, they won't always be aware of how their actions hurt others, or, in some cases, they may charge ahead anyway at the expense of others.

The church will always give equal attention to all portions of the Bible. Not even. Do you have a pet cause, something that can be backed by the Bible, which has no cheering section in your church crowd? One downfall of the Bible being so diverse and promoting so many different positive behaviors is that most churches end up consciously or subconsciously picking a few favorite core beliefs—like social justice or worship—and emphasizing those to the exclusion of others (like discipleship).

But, although the church may not always be that infallible source of hope we wish it were, I don't unravel these misconceptions in an attempt to discount the church. Rather, I expose them in an effort to help us accept that throughout the course of human history, there has never been a human or a human organization who has not succumbed to sin at one point or another. Even in the Bible, the concept of hardship and suffering is baked right in with Christ's mission. In this world, you will have tribulation, remember? So why do we have such unrealistic expectations of the church?

Am I saying that we should accept these flaws? *Not at all.* When we observe a facet of our ministry that isn't aligned with God's intentions for the church, the observation should fuel us toward change and improvement. But we should accept that these flaws will exist.

By entering this one line of programming into our minds—"churches will have flaws"—we prepare ourselves to more levelheadedly respond to the challenges that do arise.

For instance, the next time someone or something about your church gets under your skin, try to back up a little. Remind yourself that

* this is not a surprise. Churches are made up of humans and humans fail;
* every human failure is a reminder of why we need God, and the pain we experience in hard times is incentive for trying to live

out God's values with even more intensity;

* God offered forgiveness to His people and His intention was always to restore us to healthy function for the kingdom. We should follow suit;

* it is important to be objective! Just because one powerhouse person with a lot of influence around the church appears insensitive or offensive, it doesn't mean that the entire community of believers — or every Christian, for that matter — will feel or act the same way.

Lastly, remember that the Bible never claimed that the church is the hope of the world. In other words, we are not and have not ever been the superheroes in this action adventure. Jesus is the hope of the world — the one who came into the world to save mankind from perishing and the one who has overcome the world. It is only by trusting in God that we can be filled with joy and peace that allows hope to overflow from our lives to others (see Romans 15:13).

SARAH RAYMOND CUNNINGHAM is a teacher, speaker, and author. She wrote her book, *Dear Church: Letters from a Disillusioned Generation* (Zondervan, 2006), in response to watching her peer group reduce their involvement with local churches. Sarah lives with her husband, Chuck, in Jackson, Michigan. Her website is www .dearchurch.com.

PARADIME

A Christian Witness Worth More Than Twenty Cents

BILL DAHL / AUGUST 14, 2005

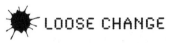 LOOSE CHANGE

If your life is anything like mine, there's loose change all over the place. It's in my wallet, the car, a mug in my office, in the bottom of storage boxes, a drawer in the kitchen, a container on an end table; it's everywhere. We've even developed phrases that contain specific references to change like, a penny for your thoughts; it's not worth a plugged nickel; it's your dime; and every time I turn around, I'm being nickel and dimed to death.

Yet what may have value in the U.S. may not be acceptable currency elsewhere. Imagine trying to pay a street merchant in Uzbekistan for an apple with five dimes, four nickels, and three pennies? Language barrier aside, no matter how hard you tried to convince the vendor that the coins you offered had value, you would likely walk away with a pocket full of loose change and a huge hankering for an apple.

We take loose change for granted in the U.S. We use terms and phrases that include the words penny, nickel, and dime throughout our lives, never giving much thought to who invented these terms, what they really mean, and whether or not they continue to serve their intended function in our society.

Christianity does the same thing. The Christian faith uses certain terms and phrases that are intended to be meaningful to all and convey value in the spiritual marketplace. The terminology that inhabits the dialogue within the Christian community is akin to loose change; everybody seems to have some, but do we ever pause to examine it to determine whether or not the sum of it all adds up to the value it was originally intended to convey? Far too often I overhear a dialogue between an evangelical Christian and a spiritual seeker that sounds like the interaction between the Uzbekistani apple vendor and an American tourist. For the Christian, maybe it's time to empty our pockets and examine the loose change we seem to be carrying around.

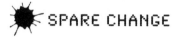 SPARE CHANGE

I saw *Batman Begins* this week. There is a line in the movie that continues to inhabit my head: "What chance does Gotham have when the good people do nothing?" This simple question got me thinking about Christianity. I started asking questions like: I wonder if you can hold a biblical worldview, be considered a good person and do nothing to positively impact your world for Christ? Which is more important, beliefs, belonging, or behaving? Is it time to take a look at the biblical worldview mantra and see how things are going?

From what I can discern, the idea of a worldview is as old as the first communication between two people, sharing their respective views on life. For evangelical Protestants, it appears that guys like John Calvin, James Orr, and Abraham Kuyper were the ones primarily responsible for getting this spiritual currency into wide circulation. Originally constructed primarily as a defense to Christianity, it has morphed into a systemic, holistic framework, within which our central beliefs and the Christian definition of reality could be articulated.[1] Orr published his *Christian View of God and the World in the Incarnation* in 1893. Carl F. Henry, Francis Schaeffer, and a few others became the primary advocates for a complete biblical vision of life during the twentieth century. Most recently, Henry Blackaby, Charles Colson, George Barna, and a whole purse full of others have safeguarded this asset.

It seems to me that this biblical worldview stuff is a lot like spare change; it's passed from one generation to the next with nary a thought about whether the sum of it all has maintained the value it was originally intended to possess. For the body of Christ, we have invested heavily in the biblical worldview fund. Our investment decision was based upon the prognostication of a substantial return on investment by presenting biblical truth as a mosaic of belief that is clear, simple, compelling, and well-packaged.[2] Yet we Christians seem to have gone well beyond this. As Brian McLaren says, we attempted to achieve "a bombproof certainty, a state of faith where all our beliefs are at rest, where everything is proven logically, where there is no dynamic tension, where everything is clear and clean and unwrinkled and in its place, like pressed shirts in a suitcase."[3] The problem is that beliefs are like essential spare change; they have different shapes, sizes, and values. When they arrive in the spiritual beliefs safe deposit box of your life, you will rarely find them in the same position when you attempt to locate them the next time you need them. They're fluid, in motion, varying in intensity and in your awareness of their presence or absence. They're alive . . . nothing like pressed shirts in a suitcase.

At this juncture, it's important to make a few things clear. I have no problem with the component beliefs identified as comprising a biblical worldview. They are unequivocally our priceless, irrefutable, irreplaceable treasure. I am most certainly not implying that we should re-examine the veracity of the fundamental biblical truths. I am not suggesting that there is anything wrong with possessing or desiring to possess a biblical worldview. I am not saying that a Christian definition of reality is not healthy and essential for a disciple of Jesus Christ today (although that reality may differ, depending upon who you speak to and exactly how they define that reality). I am taking the position that it's time to look at the returns produced by this particular investment within Christian economy by those of us who claim to possess a biblical worldview and champion its adoption by others.

I guess my concern adds up to this: If your worldview claim is that you are a dime, does that mean that you are actually composed of two nickels, ten pennies, or a nickel and five pennies? Maybe you're just another dime. From a Christian standpoint, if you refer to yourself as a Christian, does that mean that you hold the sum of all the beliefs comprising a biblical worldview? As Philip Jenkins writes, "Christianity is flourishing wonderfully among the poor and the persecuted, while it atrophies among the rich and secure."[4] Maybe this is all simply a function of socioeconomic status? Could it be that it's just spare change?

Make cents?

 SHORTCHANGED

Have you ever been shortchanged at the store? There's that essential moment when you realize, "Hey, wait a minute! Something's not right here." You immediately examine your receipt (the record of the results of the transaction) and begin counting your change. If there is a discrepancy between the results and what you received in return, well, you've been had. From a Christian perspective, let's take a look at the receipt, the record of our results from exchanging the currency of a biblical worldview in today's spiritual marketplace.

According to Charles Colson, "Genuine Christianity is a way of seeing and comprehending all reality. It is a worldview."[5] He goes on to say, "Understanding Christianity as a total life system is absolutely essential for two reasons. First it enables us to make sense of the world we live in and thus order our lives more rationally. Second, it enables us to understand forces hostile to our faith, equipping us to evangelize and defend Christian truth as God's instruments for transforming culture."[6] Translation: "You're nuts! So is the world! We're under attack, and we're going to war! Fall in, soldier!" Could this be part of the explanation of why we have so many among us who had enlisted and are now AWOL? Do you see anything in the above that talks about feeding the hungry; loving outcasts; alleviating global poverty; developing a personal, intimate relationship with the Creator of the universe; mercy; love; forgiveness; or a spiritual journey? Sounds like enlistment to me.

Colson says that the scandal in the Church is that we have failed to articulate, defend, and advance an intelligent and coherent Christian worldview.[7] Translation: The results are in. Take a look at the receipt, the record of our results. We've failed. Yep. We've shortchanged Christ. Our ability to trade the biblical worldview currency among ourselves and in the global spiritual marketplace around us has come up short—way short.

George Barna characterizes this shortchanged conundrum in the following: "American Christianity has largely failed since the middle of the twentieth century because Jesus' modern-day disciples do not act like Jesus. They fail to represent Him well not because they are incapable of Christlike behavior or out of an absence of good intentions but because they do not think like Him."[8] According to Barna's research in the U.S., only 2 percent of born-again teens and 9 percent of born-again adults possess a biblical worldview.[9]

Perhaps the following from Leonard Sweet explains the difference between what the receipt says and the change we have received from the cashier when buying into the biblical worldview: "With Christians now largely indistinguishable from non-Christians in how they live and think, there is no longer a startling freshness to the proclamation of biblical truth when it is presented as principles and propositions. How a person lives speaks much more loudly than what he or she asserts, now as always."[10]

We've been had.

 FOREIGN EXCHANGE

At present, the Chinese government will not let their currency float. This means that the yuan remains artificially valued on world currency markets. Which keeps the cost of Chinese exports artificially low. Translation: Lower costs of goods, labor, and production result in a burgeoning Chinese economy as global consumers buy more Chinese manufactured goods. Should China decide to float their currency (bowing to existing pressure from the G8 to do so), the global marketplace will establish its real value over time. Here's where it gets tricky. The question becomes, what's it really worth? What will the intrinsic value of the yuan be when it is allowed to float and is exchanged for one euro, U.S. dollar, or British pound? Answer: Nobody knows for certain. This could be either genius or economic heresy.

What's the point? What we believe about the value of the various currencies we Christians exchange in the spiritual marketplace has real consequences. Maybe we have already let the currency of the biblical worldview float. Perhaps the spiritual marketplace has established a value for this currency that is a fraction of the value we had anticipated. Certainly, in the Christian marketplace in the U.S., the production of new disciples is not booming. Maybe it's time to embrace some holy doubt. As one author says, "Sometimes doubt is actually holy—when it reveals a desire to pursue the truth, even when doing so means revising one's current beliefs."[11]

Maybe merchants and consumers just aren't accepting what we're selling in exchange for this biblical worldview product anymore. Is it possible that there has been inflation that has impacted the value of the biblical worldview currency in the global, spiritual marketplace? Has the nature of competition to purvey truth to consumers changed or intensified? Perhaps we just need more and better sales training? Those darn consumers must be the problem! Could it be that the currency of a biblical worldview can only be possessed by a select few? Maybe Christianity was never intended to be minted, circulated, and exchanged as a biblical worldview currency? Has a biblical worldview become like one of those offshore tax shelters I've read about in *Fortune* magazine? You read about this stuff in the crumpled publication stuffed in the seat pocket in front of you before takeoff, having forgotten your book in the overhead bin and climbed across folks to your window seat and buckled up. After takeoff, it dawns on you that the essential asset you've just read about, well, you've never met anybody in your circle of friends who actually has one, or at least they're not talking about it. Maybe the value of a biblical worldview is something only the experts and professionals discuss amongst themselves in lofty theological discourse that never really filters down to us common folk? When's the last time you asked a friend, how's your biblical worldview portfolio performing lately?

It's just foreign exchange anyway, isn't it?

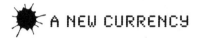 ## A NEW CURRENCY

Who would have thunk it? The formation of the European Union came before a common currency was introduced. I can recall reading the hysteria-enraged forecasts of economists and public policy pundits (the experts) predicting the utter certainty of catastrophic socioeconomic consequences if the euro was authorized to replace the currency of each member nation in the EU. To do so, each nation had to disband their deep, heartfelt attachment to the franc, lira, deutschmark, and so forth. What happened? The euro is presently worth more than the U.S. dollar. What's the point? The scenario above is a current-day example that we can belong before we issue a common currency. Is there a central issue contained within this scenario that we Christians have been banking on that now emerges as a legitimate subject for debate? Answer: Yes!

The purveyors of the biblical worldview currency have based its valuation on the gold standard that you must believe before you belong. You must buy into a certain number of component beliefs before you are really one of us. If you actually possess a nickel's worth of these beliefs and claim to be a dime like the rest of us, you're five pennies short of where you need to be. We've even developed some nice names for you like notional, nominal, church-hopping commie, seeker, or just plain lost. If you don't say that you buy into all of the life-changing tenets of our faith that make up our biblical worldview, well, we'll pray for you. Maybe you've memorized the ideas that comprise a biblical worldview. Well, more bad news, as Donald Miller says, "I don't think memorizing ideas helps anybody understand the meaning inferred in the expression of those ideas. I think ideas have to sink very deeply into a person's soul, into their being, before they can effect change, and lists rarely sink deeply into a person's soul."[12]

Hmmm. As I considered this belief-before-belong precept inherent within the biblical worldview, my mind quickly went to Matthew 4:19, the calling of Peter and Andrew: "Come, follow me." In Matthew 9:9, Jesus calls Matthew: "Follow me." In other words, "Hang out with me." Jesus knew that as He developed a relationship with Peter, Andrew, and Matthew, they would come to believe. Sounds like an invitation to a journey, a friendship, an adventure — a process. Maybe Dallas Willard is correct when he writes, "To belong is a vital need based in the spiritual nature of the human being."[13]

Frankly, the biblical worldview currency has not bought Christ much of anything constructive from an evangelism standpoint. Our primary use for the concept of a biblical worldview has been to reduce the component beliefs to questions in social research and then trumpet the results that hardly anyone possesses a biblical worldview. That's encouraging. The biblical worldview stuff has also fed "justifiable" militancy within Christianity's evangelical economy that has contributed to the marginalization of Christianity, particularly in the U.S. Finally, the biblical worldview has been at the forefront of the morphing of Christianity in the U.S. into some sort of civil religion where one must be a member of a particular partisan, political party to be considered one of Christ's. This final unanticipated consequence has cast a dark shadow over Christendom in the U.S., as those who are against an agenda of sociopolitical issues versus those who are sold out to attracting others by virtue of living lives as loving disciples of Jesus Christ. As Francis Schaeffer wrote, "Even orthodox doctrine can become merely intellectual, a final integration point, and can actually shut us off from God rather than opening the doors to Him, which it is meant to do."[14]

At this juncture, I am reminded of a few pertinent Scriptures from Romans. In Romans 14:1, Paul says, "Accept him whose faith is weak, without passing judgment on disputable matters." In the same chapter, he writes in verse 13, "Therefore let us stop passing judgment on one another. Instead, make up your mind not to put any stumbling block or obstacle in your brother's way." Perhaps we should consider the relevance of this wisdom in regard to the biblical worldview issue, as framed in the paragraph above.

I think Tony Campolo has the combination to the vault that leads to the discovery of the potential for a new currency within the Christian economy:

> The Greeks taught us that what people think and feel determines what they do. These ancient philosophers who have contributed significantly to our thinking were only partly right. While it is true that what we think and feel influences what we do it is also true that what we do influences what we think. Very often, our actions condition our thought patterns and determine our feelings more than we are willing to admit.[15]

As one author suggests, "Right relationships are not produced by right thoughts or right actions. Just the opposite. Right thoughts and right actions are produced by right relationships."[16] Maybe there's some pertinent wisdom in a phrase from Brian McLaren that says, "Sometimes belonging must precede believing."[17]

Perhaps it's time to reflect upon the fact that our collective poverty is the currency that we must cherish, versus basing the value of one's Christian witness to the world on the gold standard of a biblical worldview. As Robert Bellah wrote, "We have imagined ourselves a special creation, set apart from other humans. In the late twentieth century, we see that our poverty is as absolute as that of the poorest of nations. We have attempted to deny the human condition in our quest for power after power. It would be well for us to rejoin the human race, to accept our essential poverty as a gift, and share our material wealth with those in need."[18] Perhaps it's time to move toward a new currency, the value of which is a reflection of Christ to the world that says, "what I believe is not what I say I believe; what I believe is what I do."[19] In this sense, we come to accept that through His power, our lives become the magnetic mystery, awe, and wonder of living for what we believe, for His glory.

Perhaps becoming what you believe is a process that necessarily involves shedding beliefs that are no longer becoming. A new currency appears to be emerging within Christendom. I refer to it as embedded Christianity. This is a witness to the world that is minted on the face of the actions of our everyday lives, a reflection of the loving embrace of Christ to this, His world. Does this sound like the biblical attributes of a new currency that Christendom requires to transact His business in today's global spiritual marketplace?

 CHUMP CHANGE

Jesus was the witness to those the world considered chump change, the expendables. Now we are to be His witnesses. Yet we Christians have an indefatigable propensity to complicate our faith to such a degree that one requires an interpreter to communicate with us. Some of the elements of the Christianese vocabulary, the currency dialogue we exchange with one another and the world around us, need to be reevaluated. They are expendable, like chump change. They really serve very little useful purpose.

When I am in the Las Vegas airport departure lounge awaiting my flight, I am constantly amazed at the people who continue to plunk their coins into the slot machines that litter the area. They're trying to recoup their losses with a last-gasp opportunity to do the same thing that got them into the misery they cannot accept in the first place. Nobody wants to go home a loser. If you talk to people who live in Las Vegas, they will tell you that those airport slot machines are simply "receptacles for chump change." Maybe we need to revisit the second step in one of those twelve-step recovery programs: Come to believe that a power greater than ourselves can restore us to sanity. One of the objectives of this article is to cause us to pause, step back, and take a look at our stuff. It's not the machine that's the problem. It's us.

Remember: You and I are the chumps that He lived, died, rose, and reigns to change.

COUNTING THE COST

"Show me the money. Show me the money!" Nobody can forget those lines from Cuba Gooding Jr. in the film *Jerry McGuire*. Guess what? They're as applicable to the Christian life as they are to the expectations in the fictional portrayal of Cuba Gooding Jr. toward his agent, Jerry McGuire. We are His agents. James Emery White writes, "We will stand before God one day and give an account for our lives. . . . God will ask, 'Did you do all that you could? Did you match the intensity and fervor I brought to the cross?' People must be brought to the point of understanding that it would be a tragedy if change didn't happen. They must not simply embrace change, but cry out for it."[20]

This is why the paradime matters. Let's face it. The biblical worldview currency we are transacting is simply not producing the righteousness He desires. Yes, our God expects results, righteous results, as defined by Him. "Two bits, four bits, six bits, a dollar! All for a paradigm shift stand up and holler!" My intention has not been to devalue the currency of the biblical worldview. Yet I do believe that it is time to reconsider the wisdom of continuing to support the widespread circulation of this coinage as the gold standard upon which we witness to one another, and those around us. Do I sound conflicted? I am! Guess what? I'm not alone.

Perhaps it's time to exchange the paradime of the biblical worldview for a paradigm of deliberate, active faith. As Brian McLaren writes, "Faith involves admitting with humility and boldness that we need to change, to go against the flow, to be different, to face and shine the light on our cherished illusions and prejudices, and to discover new truths that can be liberating even though they may be difficult for the ego, painful to the pride."[21] The words of Jesus challenge us today, as the same words challenged Martha: "Do you believe this?" (John 11:26). Okay. Well, now what? As Barna says, "You and I may profess to be followers, but remember, the most significant evidence of our loyalty is not what we say but what we do."[22]

As I departed the theater after watching *Batman Begins*, a rephrasing of the line to "what chance does Christendom have if the good people do nothing?" continued to inhabit my head. Then it dawned on me, "Where's Robin?" I wonder if Jesus feels the same way about us, His disciples.

It might be time for some uncommon sense — and a paradigm that produces a Christian witness worth more than twenty cents.

God bless you.

BILL DAHL is a freelance writer and social justice advocate. Contact Bill at: wsdahl@bendbroadband.com or see his website at www .theporpoisedivinglife.com. Bill is published in numerous professional publications, magazines, websites, newspapers, and newsletters. During his business career, Bill was an executive with several FORTUNE 500 companies. Bill and his family make their home in central Oregon.

RETHINKING

WHAT IS THE CHURCH? IT seems like a straightforward enough question, yet for many on the emergent journey, it's a terribly complex one.

Historically, the Western church of the recent past has served all kinds of wonderful purposes. When books were expensive and people were illiterate, the church took on the critical role of teaching. Church buildings became campuses and pastors became teachers. When events happened in people's lives—they got married, had children, or lost a loved one—the church stepped in and guided them through. After a few weddings, baptisms, and funerals, the church became known as much for family ritual as for spiritual development. When people toiled long hours each week, isolated and distant from each other, the church facilitated social interaction and a sense of community. Everyone gathered at least once a week, and, before long, more often than that. Tuna surprise before Bible study, anyone?

Yet, although our needs as a society have changed, the church has stayed virtually the same. Despite the fact that most westerners now have unlimited access to multiple Bible translations, commentaries, systematic theologies, and countless Christian books and videos, churches still make education their primary product.

Despite the fact that people have innumerable opportunities to see and talk with other people throughout the week, churches still hype Sunday as the essential, not-to-be missed social gathering.

"You need to go back to church. Stop being frustrated, just go back to church, and it will work out," say well-meaning family and friends. But go back to what? To a teacher? To a building? To a Sunday event? Christians may say that church isn't a building, yet the discussion always seems to default there. When people use the word *church*, they almost always use it in reference to a weekly event, an address, a worship band, or a talk. Although we may tell ourselves that church is community, in actual practice, we don't seem to be sold on the idea.

In this next set of articles, the desperate cry for change is hard to miss. It's a cry not for the destruction of the church, but for its salvation. It's a cry to rethink church and challenge our underlying assumptions about our "world" and its needs. It's dissent you hear in their voices, not disloyalty. And I think it's important not to confuse the two.

Most who would call themselves emerging are committed to the church but not the institution. They're so committed that they can no longer go on pretending that everything is fine. To them, continuing to do the same things over and over again and expecting different results is, well, insanity. Desperate times call for desperate measures.

The call is not to shift a church service around, add coffee and incense, or tweak the tools currently in place. It's a call to go much deeper and rethink the whole endeavor — just what is it that God has called us to?

THE PARADOX OF A DIVIDED CHURCH CALLED TO BE RECONCILERS TO THE WORLD

ANDY MORGAN / SEPTEMBER 15, 2006

 INTRODUCTION

"The greatest barrier to the gospel in contemporary western culture is the church,"[1] or so says New Zealand theologian Mike Riddell. It is quite ironic that the very message entrusted to us by Jesus is in danger by the body created by Jesus to spread it. But what does Riddell mean? We call the church "a family" and yet, if the church were to go into therapy, it would be considered severely dysfunctional, uncommunicative, and often abusive. Riddell goes on to explain: "Our congregations function as conglomerations of committed individuals, little different from a bowling club or a Rotary club group. Most Western Christians regard even major life decisions as their private arena and would never contemplate opening the process to fellow Christians."[2]

The church has become an impersonal club—a place where you go once a week and then leave to go back to normal life. Those with needs or problems are seen as a burden because they disrupt the "normal" functional life of the church, which is about the Sunday service going smoothly and uninterrupted.

Jürgen Moltmann also raises this problem. He ponders Romans 15:7, "Receive one another, then, just as Christ also received you, to God's glory," (NET) and writes:

> Accept one another. Even in Church what hurts most is our lack of human relationships. The worship services in which we participate every Sunday morning themselves remain devoid of genuine human contact. We scarcely know each other with any genuine mutuality. We do not even consider it very valuable to create community with each other.[3]

Of course we have acquaintances with people within our churches, but these relationships tend to cease once we leave the service or meeting and go home. What is the reason for this alienation? For Moltmann the issue is that we only accept people on our own turf and view them only through our preconceptions. The conclusion of this attitude is that we do not at all seek the other but only ourselves in the other.[4] In other words, we only seek out the things in a person which we like or agree with or that are like us. The bits we dislike or disagree with or are not like us are ignored, dismissed, and avoided. This seems to affirm Aristotle's famous words "birds of a feather flock together." Yet it was not always like this in the church.

The New Testament church had no buildings, it had no clergy, it had no money, and it had no authority. People relied upon each other. To be a Christian was to go completely against the social and economic stream of the day. You would have stood out. You would have been different. People met in other people's houses. No neutral, cold, impersonal buildings, but somebody's private living space. Yes, they had faced persecution, and they would again. You did not make the decision to become a Christian lightly. Decisions were made as a community and life was lived in the context of community. And the community of believers crossed the divides of social and economic status.

✴ THE JOINING OF THE STATE AND THE CHURCH

So what went wrong? All this changed with Constantine. Christianity became vogue. Very soon it was given money and lands, a status which it had never before had. The rich began worshipping this Christian God, and appropriate people had to help them. A hierarchy soon developed. The church became institutionalized.

Whether you think Constantine was good or bad for Christianity is a matter of debate. What I would suggest is that this institutionalization was the beginning of the dysfunctional church. It made the church respectable — and that was not the function of the church. Dare I say it? Constantine let the wrong sort of people into the church!

This is not about never letting the rich, respectable, and powerful into the church. The church should cross social, economic, gender, and racial divides. However as mentioned above, the decision to follow Christ would not have been taken lightly in the first century. You risked losing everything. You risked being an outcast. Your commitment would have to be total. This is evident in the early church's practice of taking those who were interested in joining the church and putting them through a three-year course that ended in baptism. This was not a decision to take lightly or flippantly.

Constantine effectively took this away. It became fashionable to join the church, which became respectable and wealthy. Constantine began the process of the church and state coming together. Because of Constantine, the church would experience incredible influence and power in society. I believe we live with this legacy today, and for more than two thousand years we have tried to untangle ourselves from the influence of Constantine.

We have lost that radicalness of what it means to be a follower of Christ. Few of us have to lose our families, our jobs, our status, our positions, and our reputations when we become believers (though there are people today who do risk losing these things when they follow Jesus). No longer do we live or work out our life decisions within the context of the faith community.

If the church is essentially the community of God's people rather than an institution, then it is through the church as people that God is accomplishing His cosmic plan—not in the first place through organization and institutions, though these may be useful tools.

The dividing line between seeing the institutional church as a useful tool and the church as essentially the community of God's people accomplishing His cosmic plan has been lost. And this has had a serious repercussion on the church. Because the church needed to maintain an institution, the focus of the church shifted toward power and authority. In order for an organization to run well, it requires good, strong structures which are maintained and upheld.

 FOCUSING ON OUR ACTIONS

I would suggest that whatever our focus is, that will be how we act: The church's focus has been in holding onto power and influence, and that is how it has acted. The church, over the previous centuries, has been used to wielding great authority in the affairs of the world. The ecclesiastical institution has not taken kindly to being pushed to the margins. But the church is a canny player. If power could not be exercised within the society at large, it could at least be maintained within the church. How was this power maintained? Through the establishment of strong leadership and authority, and this was built upon knowledge. Theological and doctrinal emphasis grew. Those with knowledge were powerful. This has meant that now the pinnacle of the Christian life is to become a leader. Almost everything we do within church is to 'train' others in order to create leaders. This is vital in order to maintain a hierarchical structure. So a judgment is placed on you. You are either leadership material, or you're not. If you are, an investment of time, energy, and sometimes money is made into your life in order to develop your leadership skills.

If you are judged not to be leadership material, then you are asked to simply serve in the body. No investment of time and energy is made other than weekly preaching and small group gatherings. The result of this is that some members of the community of Christ became valued over other members.

This is one of the foundational reasons for the divided church; an institutionally focused church goes against Jesus' teaching that life in the kingdom of God is inextricably linked with the welfare of one's neighbor (see Matthew 16:24; John 13:14,34).

Much of the church today is not in love with its neighbor, but with words, doctrines, rational arguments, and statements about faith. Alongside the need for power and control, for many, church life has been an experience of abuse. Abusive when people are told to accept the word of those in authority and that to question those in authority is an affront to God. Abusive when any person or groups of persons claim to speak the Word of God and that claim is not subject to discernment by the wider community of believers. Abusive when decisions are made in secret by a small group of power holders, and such hierarchical rule is interpreted as being Christian. Abusive when difference is demonized, and when departure from a prescribed moralistic lifestyle is portrayed as either sinful or evil. Abusive when control is exercised to ensure the maintenance of the institution.

Abuse, be it physical, sexual, or spiritual abuse, takes place when we refuse to accept another person as Christ accepted us but use them for our own purposes. This has been the legacy of church for too long.

Moltmann's suggestion is that Romans 15:7, "Accept one another as Christ has accepted you," needs to become a new orientation in our lives, breaking through our limitations so that we can, to use his words, "spring over our narrow shadows." Indeed, this verse has incredible repercussions within the church. The church has simply not accepted people as Christ accepted us. It has not just disobeyed this verse, but it has put into practice throughout church history many plans to actively not accept certain people into the church. In this respect, much of the church has failed. And how would we fare if we judged ourselves the same way that we judge others? Maybe we would reject ourselves and fail our own criteria. If Christ accepts us while still His enemies (see Romans 5:10), then what theological excuse can be mustered that we continue to not accept others?

One of the most powerful examples comes from a book by Alan Jamieson called *A Churchless Faith*. Jamieson explores the faith of those who have left the church. He discovers a number of things which surprise him: that many who leave the church are those who have held some form of leadership and often been faithful members of their churches for between ten and fifteen years; that their faith is not just maintained but actually develops and grows once they have left the church; that the decision to leave the church community was a major, long-thought-through process. He discusses the fact that in 99 percent of the cases, the pastors interviewed never once thought that the problem for an established member of a church to leave was on the church's side. The responses were that those who left were backsliders (which defied the evidence), unstable or just troublemakers. He quotes one senior pastor as saying: "Every church needs a soundproof room where a pastor can take certain people and head butt them. Of course this would be followed by prayer."[5]

A joke maybe, but it hides the more sinister side of the church. The church which is called to be a peacemaker, a reconciler to the world, to love its neighbor, cannot bring peace to itself, both internally and between different churches. Furthermore, many leaders do not have a clue how to lead, manage, and pastor people effectively. And a large part of the reason for this is how the church views leadership.

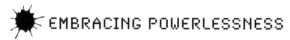 EMBRACING POWERLESSNESS

Mike Riddell suggests that it may be necessary for much of the formal structure of western Christianity to "fall into the ground and die" (John 12:24, KJV) in order for new shoots of faith to arise.[6] A total shift in focus is vital for the church—the shift away from power and authority to embracing powerlessness. Henri Nouwen writes that:

> [Christian leadership in the future] is not a leadership of power and control but a leadership of powerlessness and humility in which the suffering servant of God, Jesus Christ, is made manifest. . . . I am speaking of a leadership in which power is constantly abandoned in favour of love. It is a true spiritual leadership. Powerlessness and humility in the spiritual life do not refer to people who have no spine.[7]

Indeed, powerlessness requires a tremendous amount of courage and faith in God. There is nothing to prove to anyone. I call it the John the Baptist principle. John the Baptist had a tremendous ministry. People flocked to hear him preach and to be baptized. Then Jesus comes along. In John 3, we have the disciples of John concerned for his ministry. They say to him in verse 26, "Look, that guy you baptized is also baptizing and everyone is flocking to him!" (PAR). And John's response? Does he increase his baptism times or try and maintain his ground? No, he says, "He must become more important while I become less important" (verse 30, NET). Other translations say, "He must become greater; I must become less." (NIV).

The goal of ministry is not church growth but kingdom growth. Or even better, the goal of ministry is to become less while Christ becomes greater. It is from this place that we can again begin to be a peacemaking church, a church which brings reconciliation, because we bring only Christ not our authority or power or influence. Just as Christ emptied Himself of His divinity, humbling Himself, so we too empty ourselves of everything in order to bring Christ. If this was the principle upon which leaders operated, there would be greater unity within churches and between churches.

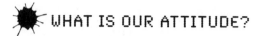

WHAT IS OUR ATTITUDE?

Philippians 2:5 begins with "your attitude should be the same as that of Christ Jesus" and goes on to talk of Jesus making Himself nothing, "taking the very nature of a servant... humbled himself and became obedient to death" (2:7-8).

This should be our attitude, yet our courses for training leaders today do not include classes on making yourself nothing or taking the nature of a servant or humility or how to humble yourself to the point of death.

This is because within the church the word *leader* is associated with power and authority; leadership is the goal and aim for a Christian in church life. My suggestion is that we cannot create leaders; leaders are called. So often we have made a person a leader because he or she is gifted in communication or charismatic in personality or great at motivating. All these gifts are valuable, but they do not make a leader. These gifts need to be developed and encouraged in creating disciples, but leadership is a calling upon a life which comes from God. Leonard Sweet, author of *Summoned to Lead* says that "the church has it all wrong. It is trying to train leaders. Instead it ought to train everyone to listen and develop their own soundtrack." We can stop putting leadership upon the pedestal of authority. Indeed, we should now remove it completely from the pedestal.

Power-based leadership is the cause of the divided church. The desire to protect and maintain authority among the congregation causes people to be neglected or used. It results in dealing suspiciously with anyone who might challenge the leadership, especially other leaders from other churches. Hence, a protective cocoon develops around the leader and the church, and anyone who tries or is perceived as trying to break into or through the cocoon is a threat and needs to be dealt with.

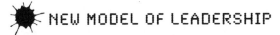

NEW MODEL OF LEADERSHIP

Henri Nouwen calls for a whole new type of leadership, free from the model of power games and focused on the servant leader, Jesus.[8] We need to recapture something of the attitude and spirit of the early church, who had servanthood, peacemaking, and loving your enemies at the core of their thinking. Yet over a period of time talk went from the converting of weapons into plough shares, spears into farmers' hooks (Justin Martyr) to picking up the ploughshare and converting it back into a sword (Augustine).

How seriously do we take the call of Jesus to love our enemy, to turn the other cheek? Surely, the argument goes, Jesus does not want us to be weak. Surely this teaching is figurative, not literal! We try to do creative accounting with the gospel, to make the gospel back our ideas for how we deal with people: We need to use violence or be aggressive towards others so how can the gospel help us? Oh yes, Jesus showed anger in the temple; he used a whip; he drove people out. This is a whip moment—this is us imitating Christ in the temple. Many times I have heard the argument from pastors that anger is acceptable because Jesus got angry, and then the pastors proceeded to act in horrendous ways toward people.

This does not mean we avoid conflict. On the contrary, as Lederach has said regarding Matthew 18, we must embrace conflict—the church does not have enough conflict in it. We must stop avoiding issues or ignoring them and hoping they will go away, and instead move toward conflict. But so often the conflict begins from someone in the congregation approaching a minister and expressing their problem. The pastor sees a threat and immediately entrenches himself in order to protect his authority. The battle lines are drawn. Pastors need to stop entrenching themselves and immediately ask the question of themselves, "Am I at fault?" "Is this a fair or true reflection of my actions?" The congregation member may be wrong. But currently, the power model dismisses any possible fault with the minister.

Jesus' motive within conflict is not to establish power but to bring peace and reconciliation, reconciliation to Himself and the Father. Should not this be our focus as well? Larry Crabb, the well-known Christian writer, had a vision of this which changed his entire outlook and ministry. His book *Connecting* describes his journey. He writes:

> The most powerful thing we can do to help someone change is to offer them a rich taste of God's incredible goodness in the New Covenant. He looks at us with eyes of delight, with eyes that see a goodness beneath the mess, with a heart that beats wildly with excitement over who we are and who we will become. And sometimes he exposes what we are convinced that it would make him turn away in disgust in order to amaze us with his grace. That's connecting.[9]

Moving from a power and authority-based leadership model to one that embraces powerlessness and a servant outlook will not be easy. Alan Krieder is right to say that we live in an environment that is not conducive to good conflict or peacemaking. As Christians we have lived within a worldview of adversarial and combative thinking. It has been so ingrained within us that to move away from it will take time, education, and example.

I tend to agree with Mike Riddell that it may be necessary for much of the formal structure of western Christianity to fall into the ground and die in order for new shoots of faith to arise. This cannot be a change which happens over months and years but decades. Even so, that does not mean that we cannot begin to model the example now.

What does embracing powerlessness as a leader look like? It looks like Jesus. It does not do things in order to gain status or recognition. Henri Nouwen captures the essence of this when he says,

> I am deeply convinced that the Christian leader of the future is called to be completely irrelevant and to stand in this world

with nothing to offer but his or her own vulnerable self. This is the way Jesus came to reveal God's love. The great message that we have to carry, as ministers of God's word and followers of Jesus, is that God loves us not because of what we do or accomplish, but because God has created and redeemed us in love and has chosen us to proclaim that love as the true source of all human life.

If Jesus emptied Himself of His divinity, humbled Himself and took the role of a servant, why should a follower and a leader of the people of Jesus be any different? Maybe it is because too many leaders do not know how to exercise healthy, intimate relationships. They have become empire builders who are unable to give and receive love. This brings me again to my suggestion that too many leaders have been created instead of having been called.

As Jesus died on the cross, the temple curtain ripped from top to bottom revealing the Holy of Holies.[10] It was symbolic. God declared in a very powerful way that no longer was access to Him done through the professional priest who restricted access to God. God is available to all. Yet the institutionalized church has, for the last 1,500 years, been trying to sew that curtain up again.

 CONCLUSION

If the church is to become a reconciler, a peacemaker, then we need to rethink how we exist as believers. Alan Krieder gives four attitudes and four skills of a peacemaker. The attitudes are humility, commitment to the safety of others, acceptance of conflict, and hope. The four skills are truthful speech, expectant listening, alertness to community, and good process (making decisions which are truthful, just, and corporate). While these skills and attitudes can be taught, they need to be lived. They must become a part of the DNA of the church leader. Powerlessness, brokenness, and servanthood are resident within these skills and attitudes.

But, fundamentally, this change needs to happen in the places where leaders are trained. There needs to be a complete reworking of what we teach and how we teach people in seminaries and colleges. For Nouwen, while powerlessness is a key to the leader of the future, the leadership of the future must also be a theological leadership. Nouwen says:

> Thinking about the future of Christian leadership, I am convinced that it needs a theological leadership. For this to come about much, very much, has to happen in seminaries and divinity schools. They have to become centres where people are trained in true discernment of the signs of the time. This cannot be just an intellectual training. It requires a deep spiritual formation involving the whole person — body, mind and heart. I think we are only half aware of how secular even theological schools have become. Formation in the mind of Christ, who did not cling to power but emptied himself, taking the form of a slave, is not what most seminaries are about. Everything in our competitive and ambitious world militates against it. But to the degree that such formation is being sought for and realized, there is hope for the church of the next century.

Nouwen is saying that theological leadership needs to be reclaimed. In the past theological knowledge was used to establish authority and power over people, creating a separation between leaders and the community — the new model of leadership takes theology and helps leaders to close the gap. Theology is not about knowledge and the mind, but about the whole person. True theological knowledge leads us to taking on the mind of Christ who emptied Himself of the privileges of His divinity. True theology should lead us to powerlessness, peacemaking, and reconciliation, formation in the mind of Christ. And while our seminaries and leadership schools are not teaching this at the moment, we need to continue to teach this message so that future seminary leaders can begin to teach spiritual formation in its wholeness.

While at Spring Harvest this year, I heard Rob Parsons say, "We must become a prodigal friendly church — a church that is so filled with the Father's love that the prodigals will return." This is a wonderful image, and I pray that this will be so.

ANDY MORGAN is a youth minister and author of two books and numerous articles. He lives in South Carolina with his wife, Kitty, and two sons.

COUNTER-CONSUMER CULTURE

MIKE PERSCHON / JUNE 16, 2005

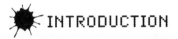 INTRODUCTION

If culture comes up in a gathering of ministers and I'm present, some-one always wants to pick my brain about what I think is permissible for Christians to listen to, view, or experience. The discussion usually centers around the statement, "our youth are being influenced by secu-lar culture" and examples of this dire influence tend to deal with some scantily clad pop star's latest video, or the latest film that is supposedly leading thousands of Christian youth down the garden path. Somehow we've confined our definition of culture to the fine arts, particularly the popular dissemination thereof.

We rarely ever imagine that culture has anything to do with the struc-ture North America is built upon: consumerism in a culture of democratic capitalism. If I mention Harry Potter or Dungeons and Dragons, I can guarantee a heated debate about how the occult is negatively influenc-ing our young people. If I mention third-world poverty or disease, I gen-erally get sentimental responses of commiseration for how awful it is, "but what can one really do about it?" After working in youth ministry for fifteen years, I have yet to meet a devout Christian turned satanist. I have, on the other hand, met more than a handful of greedy, materialistic Christian teens whose church experience not only condones their life-style and behavior, but reinforces it in the name of ministry.

I find it interesting to note that despite Jesus' proximity to Greco-Roman culture, the Gospels have no record of a condemnation of the colosseum. One might argue that Jesus' preaching ministry was for the Jews, and it would have been unthinkable for a good Jew to attend such entertainment. But Jesus didn't hold company with "good" Jews. It's likely the sinners He surrounded Himself with had experienced more than a taste of the licentious culture around them, yet Jesus makes no direct mention of it.

What He does make direct mention of, time and again, is money and the hierarchies it creates. Jesus makes many direct and aggressive statements regarding the use of money, treatment of the poor, the spiritual condition of the rich, going so far as to become physically violent over the issue of greed within the temple courts.

It's no surprise to me that the most unwelcome sermons in many churches in our culture are stewardship sermons. How do you talk about giving up all you have and selling it to give to the poor in a culture that is built upon the accumulation of, as George Carlin used the euphemism, "stuff." Preach about the evils of television until Judgment Day, and you will be applauded. Suggest that people ought to start tithing, and you get people angry at you for "telling them what to do with their money."

I am currently under the suspicion that if the collected body of Christians in North America were to actually tithe, we could likely level some of the world's debt. Whether or not it would be possible to do so is another issue, but if the stats on how many professing Christians are living in Canada and the U.S. are correct, then something is seriously wrong.

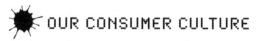 ## OUR CONSUMER CULTURE

I worked as a "fashion consultant" (the term for "jean salesperson" in a Starbuck's universe where tall is small) during back-to-school season some years ago. Being that back-to-school is easily the busiest time of the year for clothing retail, our store employed extra people to deal with the tidal inundation of parents down to their last nerve and children ready to get on it.

Staff were given their posts, since the crowd of people within the store prohibited any actual customer service. We had our five feet of responsibility; mine was one of the cash registers. There was no time for polite sentiments and customer chitchat. The order of the day was ringing customers through and getting them out the door quickly. The lineup for purchases stretched from the tills to the front of the store, and as I was madly running the scanner over price tags, making change and bagging items, I noticed a disgruntled-looking woman slowly advancing through the line. I was worried she was going to try to return something despite our No Returns sign boldly mounted on the till. When she arrived at the till, I realized that she intended neither to purchase nor return the two tank tops she had in her hands.

"Why are these tank tops two different prices?" she asked brusquely.

I looked at the two tops; one was red, the other white. The white one was regularly priced; the red, on sale. The solution seemed simple enough to me.

"Because they're different colors," I replied, managing my best customer-service smile.

"But they're the exact same item!" she said.

"I can see that," I replied.

"Well, they should be the same price."

"That may be so," I said nervously, looking at the lineup growing longer in the distance. "But they're not."

"Well can't you change it?" she demanded.

My brain wanted my lips to utter something to the effect of "If I had the power to change prices in the store arbitrarily, do you think I'd be working here on boxing day?" but what came out was more like "They do the pricing at the head office—I don't have any control over that."

She proceeded to inform me she had worked in a department store—one that had been out of business for over a decade—and their policy had been price matching.

I tried a new approach: "You know, it might be that the red one is leftover summer stock that we're clearing out, while the white one is an item we carry year round."

Undeterred, she shoved the tops at me. "Scan them to make sure."

I sighed and scanned the tops, glad to let the almighty computer register be the final arbitrator of this little skirmish. I scanned the white one: regular price. I scanned the red: still on sale. I smiled and handed the tops back to her.

"No, the prices are correct," I told her.

She made a sour face and then, her voice filled with the sort of venom I usually reserve for people working death camps, said, "Well that's just wrong."

My jaw likely dropped. Then I replied, "Ma'am, the Killing Fields in Cambodia—that was wrong. The fact that Christians and Muslims are killing each other in the Middle East—that is wrong. Third world poverty—that is really wrong. The rampant spread of STD's, the stockpiling of nuclear weapons, the fact that someone this year will invent another useless item for us to buy at Christmas 'for the person who has everything' seems wrong! But the fact that there is a ten-dollar difference in price between these two tops is not wrong; it is simply an inconvenience." (Actually, I said nothing of the sort, but it was one of those moments where I really, really wanted to.)

Between that woman and the teenagers who screamed at their parents for the *right* to purchase designer jeans, I began to think that the truly insidious nature of North American culture had less to do with Hollywood or rock music and more to do with Diesel and Mavi.

This is the culture we live in—while it may be a culture heavily influenced by the media, that media is servile to the power that runs the show. Of course, I am oversimplifying matters to some extent. The creation of culture is a complex and multifaceted process, but, for our purposes here, let us suffice to say that Western culture is driven by democratic capitalism. Sadly, it does not simply drive secular culture in the West; it drives North American Christian culture as well. This hit home when I realized how many WWJD-bracelet-wearing teens were the ones screaming for the high-priced jeans.

 ## CONSUMER CHRISTIANS

Despite Christ's overt statements regarding the poor and money (and the complete lack of even the remotest reference to music or art), Christians in North America are fixated on celebrity culture as much as any non-Christian. While poverty abounds, we stand in our designer clothes bemoaning what tramps Aguilera and Spears are becoming.

I would like to suggest (and I won't be the first to have done so) that the greatest threat to Christianity in North America is democratic capitalism. Don't get me wrong; this isn't a political statement. It's simply an observation that while we pay lip service to Jesus Christ, we bow down at the altars of Mammon.

When I was fourteen years old, a hospital burned down in Cameroon, an area in which our church's denomination had missionary involvement. The Sunday our congregation became aware of this disaster, our treasurer made an announcement concerning fundraising we had been doing for an addition to our church building. I always found it amusing that he often wore a bright green suit, the proverbial color of money. When he announced the amount we had raised for our building project, it triggered my memory, and I looked in the bulletin to verify that indeed, it was a little more than was needed to completely rebuild the hospital in Cameroon.

I sat for a while during the service, contemplating this revelation. The proposed addition to our building was an extension of our foyer and a total of three Sunday school rooms. In terms of necessity, it paled by comparison to a hospital in a third-world country. I wondered if anyone else had observed the same thing.

As the pastor stood to begin preaching his sermon, I mustered my courage and stood up from my pew, situated in the back row of the balcony. I raised my hand for good measure, to let our pastor know I wanted to say something. Like any good conservative Protestant minister, he did not acknowledge my hand. I sat back down and passed a note among the youth sitting in the balcony with me. Two of them agreed to stand with me to raise our visibility.

We stood. We raised our hands.

Still no response.

I made the suggestion we walk downstairs and stand at the back of the sanctuary. We did. We raised our hands.

No response.

By now, the service was nearly over, so we simply waited for the pastor to come out to shake hands. When he did, I told him my little epiphany: that our church family could single-handedly rebuild that hospital. He praised the idea and said he would raise it at the next church meeting. I wondered to myself if we would wait for the next church meeting to make a decision if our local hospital burned down and we didn't have the government to replace it.

The church meeting came and went, and later that year we had a new foyer with more room to mill about and chitchat following the service. I don't know what happened to that hospital in Cameroon, but I know my church wasn't part of rebuilding it.

Let me make it plain that I understand full well that as a teenager I may not have had all the facts. But as an adult I've watched families lose homes in congregations where people own summer cabins on idyllic lakes in

British Columbia. I have served at camps where staff are encouraged to wear name-brand clothing but strongly discouraged from listening to secular music. To top it all off, Christian subculture has its own massive empire of consumer items promising to improve our spirituality; if we spend more, we'll get closer to God, be it through the latest book in a series of already overstated concepts, or the latest regurgitation of worship songs five other artists already recorded.

When I look at how much Jesus talked about treatment of the poor and how much He didn't talk about the popular culture of His day, I'm firmly convinced we are constantly missing the point of what it means to be countercultural in the Western world.

GETTING COUNTERCULTURAL

Most of the curriculum I see in the Christian bookstores is still ringing the same old warning bells against premarital sex, choosing the right things to watch or listen to, and avoiding drug or alcohol use. Observing the Christian youth I've been exposed to, I find this approach is producing prudes and teetotalers who taboo Marilyn Manson, but strongly advocate owning a good pair of two-hundred-dollar Oakley shades. They can give you a number of reasons why homosexuality is a sin, but don't see the problem of their parents owning multiple leisure vehicles. Some of you reading this are wondering the same thing.

Since working with the Mennonite church, I've seen curriculum concerned with justice for the oppressed, and then seen that conviction in action. Interestingly, all the usual concerns—sex, drugs, and rock and roll—aren't an issue with these people. I have one of the most morally solid youth groups on the planet, and it's not because they don't read Harry Potter or because they don't listen to Rammstein, because they do those things. Yet, despite the presence of these supposedly diabolical influences, they constantly impress me with their Christlike lives and attitudes. I think it's because they're genuinely living lives that run counter to the root of North American culture.

I've heard it said that where other churches talk about doing the right thing, Mennonites and other churches with Anabaptist roots actually do the right thing. Unlike my own experience with trying to get my home church to see how we could rebuild a burned-out hospital, the Mennonites consistently display authentic counter–consumer culture attitudes and actions. These displays convict me and show me how far I've got to go to become truly countercultural.

The coffee in the church kitchen is fair trade, most of the people adorn themselves modestly, and name brands are a rarity unless they were bought at a discount store or secondhand. When a derelict man entered the sanctuary and shared his need for a plane ticket to Vancouver to meet a pastor who was going to help him get cleaned up, the congregation raised the money for the ticket on the spot, then organized people to take him to the airport. Those people then waited until he sobered up so that he was admissible for air travel. I was stunned, to say the least.

Even among the youth, I find myself challenged. When the tsunami hit southeast Asia last Christmas, our youth group was planning a night at a local ski hill. I challenged the group to raise at least as much money for relief efforts as they were planning to spend on rentals and lift tickets. One of my students informed me that she was planning to give seventy dollars to relief work, even before I'd made the challenge. She has no part-time job, and her family is middle income. I know this young lady well enough to know that she's giving all she has. She shamed my challenge by making a greater one. She set the bar higher than I could bring myself to. She is saying no to the consumer culture around her.

Seeking the kingdom of God, while it is certainly an internal and spiritual reality, is also something we should be doing now, in very real and tangible ways. Tony Campolo, speaking at a pastor's conference I attended, said that the kingdom of God is always in direct opposition to the Babylon or the culture surrounding the kingdom of God in exile. In North America, the kingdom of God is then in direct opposition to the Babylon of democratic capitalist consumerism.

I think it's high time we stop focusing on the red herrings and smoke-screens of fictional or perceived evils that distract us from attending to some of the very real dark and troubling evils in our culture. While it is true the Bible tells us that money itself isn't the root of all evil, it does make clear that the love of money is the root of all kinds of evil. And in North America, we've let that tree grow in our churches, spawning the evils of apathy, greed, envy, and sloth. Time to get the chainsaw and cut that tree down.

Want to be a radical counter-cultural Christian in North America? Take a stand against consumer culture, however the Lord leads you. Instead of raising awareness of the evils of some fictional book, why not work toward raising literacy in your community's schools? Instead of form-ing groups to oppose gay marriage, why not work with an AIDS clinic or involve yourself in seeking justice for this oppressed group. Get yourself a child through World Vision or Compassion International. If you already have one, get another. Sell your old PlayStation or PS2 and give the money to the poor. Then go and help your students do likewise.

MIKE PERSCHON, aka Gotthammer, is a hypercreative scholar, musician, writer, and artist, husband to Jenica, and father to Gunnar.

WAKE UP, CHURCH, AND SMELL THE COFFEE

MIKE SIMON / APRIL 16, 2007

Consider America's state of affairs.

America is one of the leading nations on the planet in marital breakup. One out of every two marriages ends in divorce. Some would say that Christian marriages have a better chance at surviving; actually that's not true. According to Barna Research Group, "the divorce rate among Christians is no different than that of non-Christians."

The definition of family is blurred. Once considered sacred, families have been relegated to a blend of options and lifestyles. How will this affect our children, our future generation?

Millions of children are aborted each year. "The United States has one of the highest abortion rates in the developed world, with women from every socioeconomic, racial, ethnic, religious and age-group obtaining abortions," says Lawrence Finer, associate director for domestic research at the Guttmacher Institute.

The National Institute of Mental Health calculates that suicides now outnumber homicide deaths by five to three. "Suicides among young people nationwide have increased dramatically in recent years. Each year in the U.S. thousands of teenagers commit suicide. Suicide is the third leading cause of death for 15-to-24 year olds, and the sixth leading cause of death for 5-to-14 year olds," according to the American Academy of Child and Adolescent Psychiatry.

Drugs, alcohol, and violence have invaded our schools, communities, and families. Every day in America, thirteen young people ages nineteen and under are killed in gun homicides, suicides, and unintentional shootings.[1] According to Laura Sullivan of National Public Radio, "Violent crime across the nation is up. For the first time since 2001, there are more murders, rapes and assaults, according to the FBI."

The Crime Clock keeps on ticking. One violent crime every six seconds, one murder every thirty-two minutes, one rape every two minutes, one robbery every forty-nine seconds, and one burglary every ten seconds.

The school dropout rate is hurting people and America. In his book *Dropouts in America*, Gary Orfield states, "Every year, across the United States, a dangerously high percentage of students, mostly poor and minority, disappear from the educational pipeline before graduating from high school. The implications of these high dropout rates are far reaching and devastating for individuals, communities, and the economic vitality of this country."

What are we going to do?

Students, teachers, parents, and people in general are disillusioned with politics, public education, economics, and the church. A major gap continues to increase between church and community. The needs of people in the twenty-first century cry out to the church to find real solutions to real problems.

Church leaders all across America are asking themselves a similar question: "Can my kind of church truly offer real solutions to the kind of real problems people face today?"

Most churches in America are hampered by stifling traditions, outdated programs, and lifeless institutional processes. Perhaps it is time for us to do whatever it takes to breathe new life into the hearts of Christians who are the church. This may require renewal, revival, or reformation.

* Renewal: to reopen the valve for creative and innovative juices to flow, impacting traditional ideas
* Revival: to restore life to that which is dying and breathe new life into old ways
* Reformation: to realign and bring relevant change to mis-aligned concepts and outdated designs

Renewal, revival, and reformation are windows of opportunity that open people's eyes to spiritual awakening, and points of entry to the pathway to transformation. This involves taking risks, embracing change, and soul-searching.

Perhaps now is the time for us to become more focused in our passionate pursuit of God and His purpose for our lives. Not self-oriented, not success-oriented, not church-oriented, but God-oriented. Perhaps we should become more serious about practicing daily spiritual disciplines, which enrich our marriages, strengthen our families, and cultivate a right relationship with God and man.

Perhaps it's time for us to quit using a marketing approach in attracting people to church, which is not a vendor of religious services, goods, or special attractions. Special events and lively entertainment may only serve in providing sporadic bursts of inspiration and enthusiasm, but they fall short in making true disciples of Jesus Christ. This happens through the transformational power of the Holy Spirit through the avenues of viable relationships.

Perhaps we Christians need to abandon our "edifice complex." As a testimony of God's influence in the community, buildings are not bad unless they provide a way for Christians to hide from non-Christians and practice a subculture that prevents them from becoming the salt of the earth and ambassadors for Christ. Buildings are a means to an end, not an end in itself. They are not monuments to our man-made egos and acquisition of resources.

The world needs Christ.

How will it find Him if Christians go to church instead of become the church? The church is the biblical community of God's people who model a Christ-oriented culture in word and deed, a testimony for the world to see and seek.

Perhaps it is time for us to engage in culture-sensitive evangelism that speaks the language of people's needs today and not religious jargon foreign to our postmodern world. People need to hear and see the language of love, hope, and faith that marks the life of a genuine Christian who is part of an authentic Christian community.

The path toward biblical renewal, revival, or reformation will not be found in any slick gimmicks, new fads, microwaveable methods, quick-success books, or man-made formulas. This path is reserved for those who "seek first the Kingdom of God and His righteousness" (Matthew 6:33, NKJV) — people with great passion for God and compassion for people.

Perhaps our only hope for change is a simple prayer: *For the sake of our nation, Lord, help us determine not to be part of the problem, but part of the solution. And let it begin with me.*

MIKE SIMON is President and COO of Simon Solutions Inc. (www .simonsolutions.com), innovators in Internet technology for churches, ministries, and nonprofit organizations. Mike has twenty-seven years of experience helping ministries grow and move forward. He and his wife, Kim, live in Florence, Alabama, along with their three children and two grandchildren.

THE DEEP
ECCLESIOLOGY OF
THE BODY

FRANK VIOLA / DECEMBER 11, 2006

My friends Andrew Jones and Brian McLaren have written about something they call "deep ecclesiology." This phrase appears to be derived from Noam Chomsky's linguistic theory of "deep semantics." Chomsky said that underlying the "surface structures" of the statements we make is a deeper and simpler structure that is ingrained in the human capacity for language.

Andrew and Brian have said that, in a similar way, there lies underneath our varying models of church a basic reality that is manifested in our historical and social settings. This notion has been termed *deep ecclesiology*.

I resonate wholeheartedly with the concept that there is a reality of the church that is higher and deeper than what typically occurs in many modern church structures. To wit, a deeper ecclesiology.

At the time of this writing, the phrase "deep ecclesiology" is still being shaped. I have shared my thoughts on this subject with both Brian and Andrew, along with some others in the emerging church conversation, so this article can be considered a stab at furthering that shaping in the public arena. I strongly believe that the underlying reality of the church is none other than Jesus Christ Himself. Not as a doctrine. Nor as a system of belief. Nor as a set of moral teachings. But as a living person who has thoughts, feelings, and volition. A living person who dwells within our

101

spirits and who can be known. To my mind, any ecclesiology that does not make Christ absolutely central in its life, mission, and expression cannot be rightly called deep.

The church is the indwelling of Christ in a group of localized people by the Holy Spirit. Those models and forms of church which best enact this reality, giving it visible expression, are adequate toward fulfilling a deep ecclesiology. Those models and forms that do not should be discarded for those that better enact it.

In this article, I shall attempt to explain how I arrived at this conclusion and what it means (at least for me) in concrete terms. I could have easily subtitled this chapter "One Man's Journey into a Deep Ecclesiology."

Shortly after I began following the Lord at age sixteen, I was introduced to something called revivalist theology. Revivalist theology was founded during the days of the English revivalist George Whitefield. It was later picked up and popularized by Dwight L. Moody.

D. L. Moody was an American revivalist who lived in the nineteenth century. Historians estimate that Moody preached the gospel to one hundred million people in his lifetime. Moody did not have television, the Internet, radio, cable TV, fax machines, MP3 players, or e-mail, nor did he put out a national magazine. He did most of his preaching on foot and preached in the open air. It has been said that Moody brought one million people to Christ.

During the period of 1870 to 1900, revivalist theology was born. And it largely came through the womb of D. L. Moody's ministry. Revivalist theology hangs on two unshakable precepts: (1) If you are lost, you must be saved. (2) If you are saved, you must win the lost. According to revivalist theology, every word in the Bible — both Old and New Testaments — hangs on these two precepts. Everything in the Bible can be juiced down to those two things.

To unravel it further, revivalist theology teaches that the only reason why you are alive today is so that you can get other people's papers in order for heaven. In fact, that is the only reason why God didn't strike you deader than a hammer after you became a Christian.

Because I had never been taught anything else, I embraced this theology hook, line, and sinker. I later came to realize that revivalist theology is untenable. It dutifully ignores 99.7 percent of the Bible. (I can only think of two occasions in the New Testament where Christians who were not apostles preached the gospel to the lost. Additionally, I cannot think of any verse in any letter in the New Testament penned by Paul, Peter, John, James, or Jude where Christians are exhorted to preach the gospel to the lost.)

Am I against revival? No. Am I against sharing the gospel with the lost? Not at all. What I am against is the tendency to take the New Testament and stretch it to the point where it fits revivalist theology. The vast bulk of the New Testament is not about winning the lost.

After I was thoroughly schooled in revivalist theology (this included knocking on doors, "four-lawing" strangers, and taking sinners down "the Romans road"), I was introduced to "the power of God." I drank deeply from the wells of a movement that obsessed over God's power. I heard sermon after sermon on the gifts of the Spirit, the recovery of the gifts, miracles, healings, signs, and wonders. I also had my share of experiences with God's power.

Today, I am a firm believer that the power of God is real and operative in our time. However, when I stood back from that season in my life, I made a few telling observations. First, most of the people I ran around with, who incessantly talked about "the power of God," were the same people who were most lacking in God's power. I saw this countless times. So much so that it became a predictable pattern.

Second, I met a few King Sauls, a few Balaams, and a few Samsons in this camp. Explanation: These three men had tremendous outward power. King Saul prophesied accurately, Balaam had an incredible gift of the word of knowledge and the word of wisdom, and Samson was unstoppable in his display of physical strength.

But there was one other thing that these three men shared. They all had defective characters in some arena of their lives. And their flesh was very much alive in those arenas. Outwardly, they had impressive gifts of spiritual power. But inwardly, they lacked something fundamental.

For me, this has been one of the greatest imponderables of being a Christian. I have personally known Christian leaders who had incredible gifts—healing, word of knowledge, spiritual understanding and insight, and the ability to preach and write with great anointing. Some of these men had very strong devotional lives and set themselves up as leaders in this area.

Yet, as dismaying as it sounds, these same men didn't have the most basic grasp of Christ in the most basic areas of the Christian life. They had profound human foibles that never traveled to the cross. The tragedy is that such men drew followings with their powerful gifts. Yet subtly, their uncrucified flesh always ended up damaging their work and causing incalculable harm to many innocent souls.

Perhaps the reason for this paradox is found in Paul's words: "For God's gifts and his call are irrevocable" (Romans 11:29). A gift is something that is freely given. It's unmerited and unearned. Once granted, it cannot be removed. A gift, then, is no measure of spirituality or character development. Neither is it an evidence of God's approval nor a sign of God's favor. It's simply a spiritual or supernatural ability given freely and irrevocably by God's grace (see Ephesians 4:8-11; Romans 12:6-8). This makes spiritual gifting a very dangerous thing. For if the vessel is not broken, or it goes off the rails later in life, the gifting becomes a liability.

The power of God that is wielded by an unbroken vessel is a very hazardous thing indeed. A destructive thing even. Not a few men have used the holy things of God for their own ends. And the result was disaster.

In one of his letters, Paul carries on rather loudly about the peril of possessing gifts of great spiritual power—including spiritual insight into the deep mysteries of God — and yet lacking some of the basic features of love, like honesty, humility, and kindness (see 1 Corinthians 13:1-3). Character, therefore, and not gifting, is the only reliable sign of God's work in a person's life (see Matthew 7:22-23).

I made another puzzling observation on this score. I noticed that so many of my fellow brethren who talked about the power of God seemed to be self-absorbed. They had an uncommon knack for talking about themselves and how God was using them with His power. Whenever they would testify, 10 percent of it seemed to be about what God was doing. The other 90 percent was how God was using them and what they were doing.

Paul of Tarsus, a man who had tremendous spiritual gifts, hardly uttered a whisper about how God used him. And the one time that he described his spiritual experiences, he was backed into a corner to testify about them. In so doing, he did two notable things. One, he used the third person to describe his revelation of the Lord. Two, he said he was speaking as a fool in detailing God's power in his life (see 2 Corinthians 12).

To put a finer point on it, I learned that those who have genuine power with God do not talk much about it. And they certainly don't talk about themselves a whole lot either. I learned that it's profoundly easy to become drunk on God's power, to become obsessed with the miraculous, to become fixated with spiritual gifting, and lose sight of Jesus Christ.

It's a perilous thing when men try to harness God. I'm a firm believer that the church of Jesus Christ has been granted enormous spiritual power. But that power is upon the church, not a set of special individuals. (We Protestants have rarely been given a corporate understanding of the Holy Spirit.) I have sadly watched the power of God be reduced to something quite common and cheap. The result: The power becomes diluted. Within the confines of the body of Christ, the power of God is safe. That's because the church is the steward of God's power. Outside of her, it becomes easily corrupted.

Am I against the power of God? Not at all. I appreciate the power of God. I am even awed by it. But I am against putting power on the throne. For that reason, I cast a cautious eye upon those who claim to have God's power.

The power of God is Jesus Christ (see 1 Corinthians 1:24). And the Holy Spirit has come to reveal, honor, and glorify Him (see John 15:26; 16:13-14). It's a fitting irony, therefore, that one of the things which will derail you and me from encountering what the Holy Spirit came to do is to seek the power of God. To put it in prescription form: Seek the power of God, and you will undoubtedly miss Christ who embodies that power.

After that season in my life, I was sold a different bag of Christian goods. I ended up on the eschatology train. Eschatology is the study of things to come—the study of end times. When is Jesus Christ going to return? When is Russia going to invade Jerusalem? What is the meaning of the ninth toe on the foot of the beast in the book of Revelation? When does Daniel's "seventy weeks" begin? Who is the false prophet? And of course, who is the antichrist and exactly what is the mark of the beast?

Open admission: I caught eschatology fever. I was bitten by the Rapture bug. I began studying the visions of Daniel and Revelation, making charts, plotting graphs, mapping out the movements of the antichrist, the false prophet, Gog and Magog, and so on.

Attention young Christians: You can get ridiculously obsessed with Rapture fever! I was taught, "This is important. We have to know prophecy. We must study prophecy. Ninety percent of the Bible is prophecy. We have a duty to understand it." Let me confess. I was pathetically into eschatology. So much so that I could discuss it for hours with wild-eyed fascination.

But I made a discovery. All of those hours I spent poring over Daniel, Ezekiel, and Revelation, trying to put the end-time puzzle together, did not help me one iota to come to know my Lord better. It was largely an academic, intellectual exercise. And a sterile one at that.

The result: I stopped studying end-time prophecy.

After I got off the eschatology bandwagon, I was introduced to something called "Christian theology" and "Christian doctrine." I was taught that the most important thing that God wants for His people is that they know and embrace "sound doctrine." So I rigorously studied the Scriptures, along with the views of Calvin, Arminius, Luther, and many contemporary theologians and scholars.

In my early twenties, I was attending various Bible studies — each sponsored by different denominations and movements. There I would engage in the usual shrill disputes over doctrine with my Christian brothers. I will shamelessly admit that I enjoyed the mental stimulation of sharpening my doctrinal sword on the side of someone else's head.

But during that season, I made another discovery. Namely, that Christian doctrine can make a person downright mean. I observed that the men who were the most schooled in Christian doctrine and the most concerned about sound theology did not resemble Jesus Christ at all in their behavior. Instead, they seemed to center their lives on making the unimportant critical. The spirit of the Lamb was altogether missing. They were harsh personalities who appeared to almost hate those with whom they disagreed. Granted, there is a doctrine in the New Testament. But majoring on Christian doctrine and theology can turn Christians into inquisitors.

Am I against doctrine? No, sir. Am I against theology? No, ma'am. But I do not advocate an overemphasis on it. Consequently, I came to the place where I was compelled to lay down my doctrinal sword, for, like Peter, I had been cutting people's ears off with it.

I recommend that you study church history. It will make you cry. Our forefathers drew their swords against one another, spilling their blood over doctrines. Peripheral doctrines at that! They crossed swords over their private interpretations of Scripture, and it often ended in bloodshed. Again, majoring in doctrine can make a Christian vicious. History bears this out.

After I dropped pursuing doctrine and theology, I became involved in a lot of other Christian "things." I majored in holiness, believing that it was the central theme of the Bible. I then majored in faith and learned the principles of walking in and living by faith. I became deeply involved in worship and praise — deeming both to be the central desire of God. Then it was ministry to the poor. Then personal prophecy.

After that it was Christian apologetics. My venture into apologetics led me to debate with the president of the American Atheist Association in the city where I lived. I was twenty-three years old at the time. I studied the apparent contradictions of the Bible and resolved many of them. (Today, I am perfectly content to leave them unresolved!) While it was great fun watching my atheist opponent squirm, the thrill soon wore off. While he didn't convert to Christ, he had to rethink his understanding of what a Christian was. Even so, I suspect there was little eternal value that came of it.

Enough of the historical narrative. Here is my point. In the first eight years of my Christian experience, I learned to major in a slew of Christian things. And that is my point . . . they were things!

All of the churches and movements I was involved in had effectively preached to me an "it." Evangelism is an it. The power of God is an it. Eschatology is an it. Christian theology is an it. Christian doctrine is an it. Faith is an it. Apologetics is an it.

I made the striking discovery that I don't need an it. I have never needed an it. And I will never need an it. Christian its — no matter how good or true — eventually wear out, run dry, and become tiresome.

I don't need an it; I need a Him!

And so do you!

We do not need things. We need Jesus Christ.

Everything in Scripture — every book, every story, every teaching, every theme, every letter, every verse — all of the arrows point to Him.

- "You search the Scriptures because you think they give you eternal life. But the Scriptures point to me!" (John 5:39, NLT).
- "And beginning with Moses and all the Prophets, he explained to them what was said in all the Scriptures concerning himself. . . . Then their eyes were opened and they recognized him" (Luke 24:27,31).
- "He said to them, 'This is what I told you while I was still with you: Everything must be fulfilled that is written about me in the Law of Moses, the Prophets and the Psalms.' Then he opened their minds so they could understand the Scriptures" (Luke 24:44-45).

To be truly Scriptural is to be Christological, for Jesus Christ is the subject of all Scripture. This discovery changed my life.

My journey didn't end there, however. Around the same time, I made another life-altering discovery. It was this: that Jesus Christ is the embodiment of all divine things. My eyes were opened to see that Jesus Christ is salvation. Jesus Christ is the power of God. Jesus Christ is holiness. Jesus Christ is doctrine. Jesus Christ is the living incarnation of everything that is spiritual!

You can chase things until you are blue in the face. And there will always be some Christian who is peddling a new it or a thing upon which to center your life. Warning: If you buy into it, you will most certainly miss Him.

When I realized that Christ was everything in the Christian life and that the Father had put all spiritual things into Him, it radically changed my life. Gone were the days where I sought "things." Gone were the days where I chased after Christian truths, doctrines, and theologies. A new chapter had opened where I began to seek Christ Himself. I sought to be drowned in the face of the knowledge of my Lord. For I discovered that in Him exists everything that I needed.

God's object from first to last is His Son. It is Christ — and Christ alone — that God the Father desires for His people. I had grossly confused spiritual growth with acquiring spiritual things. So I went about pursuing spiritual knowledge, spiritual virtues, spiritual graces, spiritual gifts, and spiritual power. I later discovered that spiritual growth is nothing more than having Christ formed within (see Galatians 4:19). When we are saved, Jesus Christ is begotten in us. He then grows in us. Spiritual growth, then, is nothing more than knowing Him and allowing Him to grow in us.

Upon reflection, it seems that many Christians regard salvation, evangelism, peace, power, holiness, joy, service, church practice, ministry, and doctrine as simply divine "things" — all detached from the living person of Christ and made to be something in and of themselves.

But God never gives us spiritual things. He never gives us virtues, gifts, graces, and truths to acquire. Instead, He only gives us His Son. He gives us Christ to be all things for us.

Consequently, Jesus Christ is the embodiment of all spiritual things. He is the substance of all divine realities. He is the incarnation of all spiritual virtues, graces, gifts, and truths. In short, God has vested all of His fullness into His Son.

In other words, Jesus Christ not only reveals the way to His people, He is the Way. Jesus Christ not only reveals the truth to His people, He is the Truth. Jesus Christ is not only the giver of life, He is the Life (see John 14:6). Put another way, Christ is the embodiment of all that He gives! He is All and All. That is, He is everything to everyone who has received His life.

- Jesus Christ is hope (see 1 Timothy 1:1).
- Jesus Christ is peace (see Ephesians 2:14).
- Jesus Christ is wisdom (see 1 Corinthians 1:30).
- Jesus Christ is redemption (see 1 Corinthians 1:30).
- Jesus Christ is holiness (see 1 Corinthians 1:30).
- Jesus Christ is righteousness (see 1 Corinthians 1:30).

Hope is not a thing to be sought; it is a person. Peace is not a virtue to be obtained; it is Christ. Righteousness is not a grace to be asked for; it is Christ, and on and on. One is a spiritual "thing." The other is the Lord Himself. To put it in a sentence, Jesus Christ is not simply the giver of gifts, He Himself is the gift.

Spiritual progress, therefore, is tied up in knowing Christ as our all. Spiritual growth takes place when we take Christ as our portion to be all things for us. Greater Bible knowledge will not do this for you. Increased religious activity or spiritual service will not do this for you. Neither will spending more time praying. Only a revelation of the vastness of Christ can meet the bill.

As I survey the landscape of modern Christianity, it seems to me that spiritual things and objects have replaced the person of Christ. The doctrines, gifts, graces, and virtues that we so earnestly seek have substituted for Jesus Himself. We look to this gift and that gift; we study this truth and that truth; we seek to appropriate this virtue and that virtue, but all along we fail to find Him.

When the Father gives us something, it's always His Son. When the Son gives us something, it's always Himself. This insight greatly simplifies the Christian life. Instead of seeking many spiritual things, we only seek Him. Our single occupation is the Lord Jesus Christ. He becomes our only pursuit. We do not seek divine things, we seek a divine person. We do not seek gifts, we seek the giver who embodies all the gifts. We do not seek truth, we seek the incarnation of all truth.

God has given us all spiritual things in His Son. He has made Him to be our wisdom, our righteousness, our sanctification, our redemption, our peace, our hope, and so on. Recognizing that Jesus Christ is the incarnation of all spiritual things will change your prayer life. It will change your vocabulary and the way you think and talk about spiritual things. And it will ultimately change your practice of the church.

To put it candidly, you will never have an authentic experience of the body of Christ unless your foundation is blindly and singularly Jesus

Christ. Church life is born when a group of people are intoxicated with a glorious unveiling of their Lord. The chief task of a Christian leader, therefore, is to present a Christ to God's people that they have never known, dreamed, or imagined. A breathtaking Christ whom they can know intimately and love passionately. The calling of all Christian servants is to build the *ekklesia* upon an overmastering revelation of the Son of God. A revelation that burns in the fiber of their beings and leaves God's people breathless, overwhelmed, and awash in the glories of Jesus.

From God's standpoint, the church's center of gravity is Jesus Christ. When a church is centered on the ultimacy of Christ, it no longer chases Christian things or its. Knowing Christ, exploring Him, encountering Him, honoring Him, and loving Him becomes the church's governing pursuit. Rightly conceived, the church is a group of people who have been immersed and saturated with a magnificent vision of Jesus Christ and who are discovering how to take Him as their all together. This discovery lies at the heart of a deep ecclesiology.

"I count all things but loss for the excellency of the knowledge of Christ Jesus my Lord: for whom I have suffered the loss of all things, and do count them but dung, that I may win Christ. . . . That I may know him, and the power of his resurrection, and the fellowship of his sufferings . . ." (Philippians 3:8,10, KJV).

To summarize, before we can understand what the church does, we must first understand what the church is. We must unearth the ontology — or the essence — of the church.

According to Scripture, the church is not a human creation. Instead, it existed before creation (in Christ) and before culture began. God created the universe for the church and not the other way around. To put it another way, God created the universe so that He might have a bride, a body, a house, and a family. This is the metanarrative that permeates the entire Bible.

Consequently, the church was not an afterthought nor a means to an end. The church is the end! God's ultimate purpose is to transform the world into the church—which is Jesus Christ in corporate human expression. This does not suggest that the church should not find ways to contextualize the gospel to the present culture. It should. But it should not ape the culture and violate its DNA in the process.

A deep ecclesiology, then, honors all Christians regardless of their religious pedigree. It esteems all Christians wherever they are on the basis that they are membered to Jesus Christ. Those models of church which make Jesus Christ central in its life, its mission, and its expression are faithful to a deep ecclesiology. Those models which clash with the church's DNA—which is Christ—are incompatible with a deep ecclesiology.

I shall close with the words of A. B. Simpson, which are fitting:

Once it was the blessing, Now it is the Lord;
Once it was the feeling, Now it is His Word.
Once His gifts I wanted, Now the Giver own;
Once I sought for healing, Now Himself alone.

Once 'twas painful trying, Now 'tis perfect trust;
Once a half salvation, Now the uttermost.
Once 'twas ceaseless holding, Now He holds me fast;
Once 'twas constant drifting, Now my anchor's cast.

Once 'twas busy planning, Now 'tis trustful prayer;
Once 'twas anxious caring, Now He has the care.
Once 'twas what I wanted, Now what Jesus says;
Once 'twas constant asking, Now 'tis ceaseless praise.

Once it was my working, His it hence shall be;
Once I tried to use Him, Now He uses me.
Once the power I wanted, Now the Mighty One;
Once for self I labored, Now for Him alone.

Once I hoped in Jesus, Now I know He's mine;
Once my lamps were dying, Now they brightly shine.
Once for death I waited, Now His coming hail;
And my hopes are anchored, Safe within the vail.

FRANK VIOLA is one of the most influential figures in the contemporary house church movement. For the last twenty years, he has been gathering with organic house churches in the United States. Frank is an internationally known speaker, a nationally recognized expert on emerging trends for the church, a house church planter, and the author of eight revolutionary books on radical church restoration, including *Pagan Christianity*, *God's Ultimate Passion*, *The Untold Story of the New Testament Church*, *Rethinking the Wineskin*, and *Who is Your Covering?* Learn more at www.frankviola.com.

EXPERIENCING

I HAVE A FRIEND IN the Bahamas named Clint. Every year he hosts a gathering of an eclectic, international group of people: thinkers, pastors, authors, musicians, social activists. Clint is the kind of guy who is full of life. He's energetic but, like the island where he lives, he has a calming influence on those around him. He knows how to set others at ease.

The first time I attended one of these gatherings, Clint gave a run-down of the itinerary for the weekend. I thought I heard him say something about sharks, so I asked him to clarify our planned underwater activities. Sure enough, he explained that the following day we would head out to swim with the sharks. Literally. Now, if anyone had told me before I went to this gathering that I'd be swimming with sharks I would have said he was crazy. But with my friend Clint jumping in first, I agreed to go.

I can't adequately describe the feeling of sitting in the boat, dressed in snorkel gear, while the tour guides throw chum into the water and then tell you, "Go!" Let me just say my heart was pounding, my breathing was heavy, my palms were sweaty, and I assumed I wasn't going to make it out intact. Once in the water, I was face-to-face with eight-foot sharks swimming all around us with no steel bars, no glass, no netting in between.

To make the story short, it was an amazing experience and I emerged safely with a tale to tell. In fact, it was such a great experience, I'm going to recreate it for everyone who comes to the Soularize event this year.

Why? Because we all have assumptions that just aren't true. No matter how many academic conversations we have or PowerPoint presentations or studies we see within the safe confines of our homes or our familiar belief systems, we can't fully examine our assumptions without testing them, without jumping into the waters of experience.

Asking questions, facing fears, engaging with others, wandering the back roads — even if the direction seems to be headed into dangerous waters — that's what the writers are doing in this next set of articles.

CULTURAL REFUGEES IN GAY NIGHTCLUBS

PETER J. WALKER / JANUARY 3, 2006

Things don't always work out like the snapshots in my head. I tend to idealize super-spiritual events and pray for ground-shaking God moments, but they don't always come. Sometimes I'm left silent, pondering, asking God which way I should turn. Two weeks ago, I went up to Portland for a friend's birthday. I knew there would be some homosexuals and Buddhists, liberals and Darwinists there — all the most interesting kinds of people I seldom encounter in my church.

I planned on bringing up an assignment I was working on for a seminary class at George Fox: designing a postmodern church plant. In my mind I envisioned exciting, stimulating conversation, delving into the very nature of faith and community. I wondered about the fascinating perspectives I might encounter. My brain orchestrated all sorts of potential dialogue strings.

Little of the spiritual talk I had hoped for took place. Whether led by fear, complacency, or the Holy Spirit, I couldn't find the proper time to introduce my class project. Instead, after cutting up a cake, we went out for drinks and somehow ended up at a gay nightclub.

And when I say "gay," I mean really, really gay!

We made our way through a large, open bar area that connected to a dance floor. Men were everywhere, dancing, laughing, and drinking; an occasional woman stood out prominently in a few of the groups. We entered a lounge area in the back that was fairly well lit, comfortable, with couches, cushy chairs, and even a Christmas tree.

What struck me, sitting there with my three straight friends (our gay companions stayed on the dance floor), was the unspoken aura that filled the room. It wasn't happiness or fun or even sadness. It was more like partial relief. A tense undercurrent still seemed to permeate the air. These men looked and acted like battered, distrustful refugees.

As we talked, I watched two young men enter, glancing around the room. They said nothing to each other as they carefully sat down in overstuffed chairs facing one another. I thought I caught a brief look of ease as they began to adapt to their surroundings, and if I could have put words to what I witnessed, they would have said, "I think it's okay. We're safe now."

I was in a bomb shelter. A refugee camp. A place where the wounded and broken came to hide and confide, to find solace or escape.

You can say what you want to about the theology or legality of homosexuality. I'm initiating no such discussion. Instead, I raise the question: If not a gay bar, where could these men go to be broken, wounded, and imperfect? Again, regardless of theology, can the church be a place for solace? Can we let these hurting souls recoup in a safe, respectful, gentle atmosphere? Or must we break down their walls of sin before we allow any relaxation or "decompression" to occur?

I don't think a gay nightclub is a good place for a gay man to find healing, wholeness, or safety. Yes, he can be gay without fear of judgment in such an environment, but no one can be transparent in a meat market — gay or straight. No one can put down the facade when they're being checked out and sized up by potential suitors (one of the reasons I think many church youth and young adult groups are so dysfunctional — but that's a whole separate can of worms!).

Maybe we could take a little break from the tired gay topic in church. Maybe if we let people come in and feel safe, the Holy Spirit would do some amazing, powerful things. Maybe we jump the gun on the Holy

Spirit. Maybe we don't trust the Spirit to speak without our vulgar voices chiming in at a whim.

I don't think this issue is simple or black-and-white. I don't even think it's ready to be resolved in our Christian culture yet. I also don't think it would be appropriate for every Christian to walk into a gay bar—maybe it wasn't appropriate for me. But right or wrong, I'd rather take chances to discover these refugees in hiding than stay so safe that I never meet the people I once called "lost."

PETER WALKER is a student at George Fox Seminary, part-time preacher, and a charter contributor at Wikiletics.com. He is featured in the upcoming *Church of the Perfect Storm*, edited by Leonard Sweet. Peter lives in Oregon with his wife and their agnostic cat.

INTERNATIONAL CHURCH

Postmodern Model?

MIKE STANTON-RICH / NOVEMBER 29, 2002

I am the pastor of an international, interdenominational congregation in Kobe, Japan. I serve a very diverse congregation. On the whole they are young compared to the average church in the U.S., but they are older than the average postmodern church.

On any given Sunday we'll have fifteen countries represented, six or eight languages spoken, and any number of misunderstandings because of language, culture, and faith differences. My worship leader claims to be a premillennial, pretribulationist. The family that always sits near the front was baptized in the Church of England. My lay leader is a former Mormon, now Presbyterian, while one of our key leaders grew up in the Orthodox tradition. Let's just say that there is never a dull moment here.

There are numerous pastors serving churches just like this one all over the planet. When we get together, we talk about these churches being a training ground for the postmodern church.

Worship. In most cases, we have gotten over the idea that it is traditional or contemporary. Even though we might still call the services by that name, my "contemporary" service would not impress many folks as one. There aren't many tunes over twenty years old, but the "liturgy" is strictly 1950s because it resembles what a majority of folks' churches call contemporary back home. The same would be true of our traditional service, which this past Sunday included images, video, as well as some experiential aspects. When we have communion every month, I am convinced that we are melding ancient and future together like few mainline churches do it in the U.S.

Leadership. This is one of the more interesting aspects of an international church. People are not in the community long enough to become entrenched. Most people stay for less than three years on overseas assignments, so every year finds a new slate of officers. Even the pastor is not entrenched—the longest tenure of any pastor at the church in 130 years was six years. This leads to a different kind of leadership than might be expected in a typical church back home. We have to spend time working quickly in teams and solving problems in teams. Even though there is the desire from some to have a CEO pastor, there is no real practicality in that notion. Most of these folks work in companies that essentially are using team model approaches, and it only makes sense to do it in church as well.

Living in a non-Christian culture. In the U.S. they bemoan the fact that Christian hegemony is in its last days. In many of the countries where there are international churches, there never was a Christian society. In Japan, less than 5 percent of the country identifies itself as Christian, and less than 2 percent of the population is in church over the weekend. It takes great perseverance to be a Christian in this context, so the level of commitment among the native Japanese is amazing. Every Sunday when this hard-to-find church, with very little parking and serious space issues, is filled to overflowing with a mix of a wide variety of folks, it is a testimony to God's grace and sense of humor. People do not show up to be inconvenienced without being a little countercultural.

Service and Mission. For the most part, these churches are beyond throwing a few dollars at a project (though they will do it). There is a need to be hands-on responsible. So we send teams to Thailand to build houses, teams to the Philippines to help orphanages and children's ministries. We have sent groups to assist with the rehabilitation of prostitutes, and we regularly help the homeless in our own community. And in those cases when money does leave their pockets, they make it possible to bring people from the ministry to the church for promotion and education. There is this sense that mission and service brings meaning and requires some kind of sweat equity.

HOW THE INTERNATIONAL CHURCHES DIFFER

Financial issues. One thing that international churches struggle with constantly is the predicament of being prosperous. The financial compensation of these young executives makes the head spin. I would generally have to work three years to make the salary of my average member, and I get paid better than the average worker in Japan. This does not appear to be the case in most postmodern churches in the U.S. The majority of folks in international churches have already given themselves over to a culture of success, so their experience of a Christian walk will be much different than many in the U.S. How many of your parishioners struggle over whether to go to Thailand or Bali for Christmas break?

Married with children. This group of postmoderns got careers, married, and had children earlier than many of their counterparts back home. I rarely hear the story of someone still living with parents at age thirty (though it is occurring more in the Japanese culture these days). Very few of my parishioners have forsaken the success culture to pursue art or music for a period of time. I may be one of the oldest parents among my son's peers and may have one of the most countercultural jobs in the community—I'm a pastor. Think about that.

A frantic, time-strapped group of people. This may be common everywhere, but I have never witnessed the intensity of the frantic pace that this group keeps. The spreadsheets that these corporate wives keep that they call calendars blow the mind. Following four grueling volunteer days at the school, church, community center, and apartment complex, these same women will board a plane and spend the weekend shopping in Hong Kong for rest and relaxation. Their husbands are much worse. Many live within walking distance of their headquarters for convenience, then proceed to work around the clock most of the week, travel 50 percent of the month, and then to relax, take the family away to another country as often as possible. I have discovered that when somebody commits to a church meeting, it is a real commitment.

So there's a bird's-eye view of ministry in an international church. It is postmodern and it isn't. Is it a model for the future? Only time will tell.

Curator's Note: Since the beginning, TheOOZE.com has offered articles and message boards for the community to describe and discuss emerging thought. In 2006, we added a feature to TheOOZE.com that allows readers to post comments to articles directly, bringing new opportunity for interaction with the author and other readers. For the following article, we have included many of the comments originally posted with it to show the type of interplay that often occurs as the community engages with an author and topic.

A TINY FEMALE EMERGENT VOICE

Why I Won't Ask for a "Seat at the Table"

LISA DELAY / OCTOBER 24, 2006

The emergent conversation was a breath of fresh air I delightfully stumbled onto and into shortly after I read Donald Miller's *Blue Like Jazz*. I realized there were more people out there than I ever realized who were thinking about Christianity like I was. It was sort of like the 1977 *Close Encounters of the Third Kind* movie, where different people are getting the same messages and find each other, only with fewer extraterrestrials and no repeating five-note jingle communiqué.

Things got even better. I found the emergent village. As I looked further, I discovered a scant few women were making contributions in a group called "emerging women." Before then it seemed you needed to be a green, single, white male and preferably clergy or risk being a sore thumb in heels. "What a relief!" I thought, until I realized contributions were dominated by ordained, "liberal" female pastor voices. Not that I didn't want to hear from them. I loved it. These brilliant ladies are inspirational!

Still, I kept thinking how could this amazing conversation seem so wonderful, so Jesus-inspired yet only include a representative sliver of female Christendom? Where are the everyday gals? The emerging ladies often weren't really like me. I sat on my end of the conversation at my keyboard with no Masters of Divinity, no congregational authority, no PhD, and sort of scratched my head. I'm more of a progressive (but not truly left-leaning), married with children, disciple maker, friend, writer, speaker, artist. I'm nobody.

Then I saw the conference information for "A Seat at the Table." Although in some ways this event looked to be promising, it made me think, "what is all this business about clamoring for a seat, ladies?"

I immediately thought of the Gentile woman of Matthew 15 fame:

> A Canaanite woman from that vicinity came to him, crying out, "Lord, Son of David, have mercy on me! My daughter is suffering terribly from demon-possession."
>
> Jesus did not answer a word. So his disciples came to him and urged him, "Send her away, for she keeps crying out after us."
>
> He answered, "I was sent only to the lost sheep of Israel."
>
> The woman came and knelt before him. "Lord, help me!" she said.
>
> He replied, "It is not right to take the children's bread and toss it to their dogs."
>
> "Yes, Lord," she said, "but even the dogs eat the crumbs that fall from their masters' table."
>
> Then Jesus answered, "Woman, you have great faith! Your request is granted." And her daughter was healed from that very hour. (verses 22-28)

What emerges from this story is the reward of humility and faith. I believe Jesus made an example out of this woman for us as emergent women to follow. How lovely is the one in whom the Lord finds favor, the lowly ones!

Another "seat at the table" reference surfaced from none other than Jesus again. Starting in Luke 22:24, the passage reads,

> Also a dispute arose among them as to which of them was considered to be greatest. Jesus said to them, "The kings of the Gentiles lord it over them; and those who exercise authority over them call themselves Benefactors. But you are not to be like that. Instead, the greatest among you should be like the youngest, and the one who rules like the one who serves. For who is greater, the one who is at the table or the one who serves? Is it not the one who is at the table? But I am among you as one who serves." (verses 24-27)

Wow. This struck a chord too. I am one who serves. Sometimes we don't know the names of those who serve us, but in God's economics, these have the most value. It was a challenge to me to serve this conversation and not strive for a stake in it. Jesus keeps bringing up this point. It's hard to ignore it. I'm even writing a book about it, because it's vital to an authentic life of grace.

I don't think begging for a seat at the table in the conversation will do as much good as being content to squat on the floor with the crumbs, ladies. Doesn't that sound humiliating? If that is the posture we take, it is the one most closely aligned with that of the One we follow. The lower posture is the higher path. Are we willing to be that and to do that? I don't think many of us are, or not enough of us. It goes against many feminist ideals and bids for equality. It goes against long-fought-for places in society.

The egalitarian nature of the conversation is such a breath of fresh air to me. But it's not pollutant-free. Jesus prized women. Back then they were the lowest in society, even lower than male children. Sometimes the dogs ate before them. Jesus showed the kind of love women need to show men even when their voices aren't heard; even if men won't show us the same love in return. Men following Jesus may not be fully sensitive, and women following Jesus may be harping on fairness. Here is the big point: The strength and nexus of this emergent conversation with legs, I believe, comes from something I am hearing too little of and that is the chief and defining characteristic of Jesus: humility.

Here is something for all of us to include in our lives and conversation communities:

> When he noticed how the guests picked the places of honor at the table, he told them this parable: "When someone invites you to a wedding feast, do not take the place of honor, for a person more distinguished than you may have been invited. If so, the host who invited both of you will come and say to you, 'Give this man your seat.' Then, humiliated, you will have to take the least important place. But when you are invited, take the lowest place, so that when your host comes, he will say to you, 'Friend, move up to a better place.' Then you will be honored in the presence of all your fellow guests. For everyone who exalts himself will be humbled, and he who humbles himself will be exalted."
>
> Then Jesus said to his host, "When you give a luncheon or dinner, do not invite your friends, your brothers or relatives, or your rich neighbors; if you do, they may invite you back and so you will be repaid. But when you give a banquet, invite the poor, the crippled, the lame, the blind, and you will be blessed. Although they cannot repay you, you will be repaid at the resurrection of the righteous." (Luke 14:7-14)

Honor at the table is probably not what you think it is or hope it will be. But look to Jesus! What a beautiful picture Jesus is for us. He is the perfect example. Jesus was a man, a son of royal king David, and, of course, please don't forget the biggie, He was equal with the God of the universe. He had plenty of reasons not to concern Himself with being humble in heart, but look closely at Matthew 11:29. Here is the archetype from which to learn: Jesus says, "Take my yoke upon you and learn from me, for I am gentle and humble in heart, and you will find rest for your souls."

That's all we need to remember, my ladies, my sisters. I won't ask for a seat at this emergent table. Sure, I'll come if I'm invited, but I will do fine with the crumbs. I will that the name of Jesus be glorified. The way of my Lord is made more as I am made less.

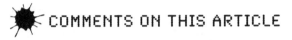**LISA DELAY** is represented by literary agent Chip MacGregor. Lisa is a graduate student, concentrating in spiritual formation, at Evangelical School of Theology in Myerstown, Pennsylvania, and archives articles at www.lisadelay.com. Her emergent blog is www.emergingPA.blogspot.com.

COMMENTS ON THIS ARTICLE

Hi Lisa,

I really enjoyed your article, especially the way you join your words and heart with Scripture to bring your message to life. A good reminder for me. I laughed when you referred to yourself as a married with children, writer, speaker, artist without an MDiv or PhD, because my gifts and situation are similar, although you are a bit farther on your journey. I am curious what experiences you have had with being left out of the emerging conversation and your observations about this dynamic in general. Do you think men are reticent to hear from women or that "normal gals" are intimidated by men who speak eschatologicalese and hold fancy degrees?

Also, I think practicing humility must be balanced with working toward inclusion and justice for our sisters and daughters. Jesus was willing to suffer, but He was not willing to accept the status quo. How do we practice humility, grace, and justice in the name of Jesus?

Blessings, Jemila

✹ ✹ ✹

Hi there, Jemila.

You ask some good questions.

I don't suppose I've felt "left out" in a sense that there has been some overt message that says, "Stay away." Prominent leaders—if you can really called them that specifically—of the emergent movement are noticing the dearth of divergent voices in what is suppose to be a dynamic and diverse conservation about Christian spirituality. There is some effort to be more accommodating as well, which is nice to see. One disappointing and paradoxical aspect is that a movement (emergent) that is by nature, nurture, and period in history more egalitarian is also solidifying into a unilateral one.

I come from a background of subjugation, not grace, from most of my church experiences, so the emergent movement seems sweet and filled with the presence of the Holy Spirit and Christ's character in comparison. Heavy-handed enough to be in error, the reluctance of men from many mainline denominations and backgrounds marginalizes female points of view and teaching and stiff-arms insights of spiritually mature women. Even in contemporary circles I've noticed that men's strongly favoring the spiritual insights of men over women has been the norm, except in liberal churches. This seems to be to a waste of gifts and resources for the body of Christ.

I think many men, and nearly all mature and spiritually grounded men, in my daily interactions are willing to hear my insights. Whether they value them on par with men is hard to quantify. I don't think it's important to know because it's not edifying. It probably depends on both the manner in which I present insights/ideas, as well as the individual's bent, or even the mood of the male listener.

I personally don't feel intimidated by fancy degrees (I can just speak for myself; other women may feel intimidated)—but I *do* believe knowledge most often puffs up. The Bible is true after all, and it makes mention of this potential and common trap. It's a trap I can succumb to also, even without a fancy title, trust me! (If we're honest about it, we can *all* fall prey.) I've learned we must be in continual Spirit-led awareness and submission to God to avoid a posture of pride because pride is our default setting.

My message is that the approach to being heard mustn't be how we would, typically, try to attain it. It must emulate the paradox of Christ's servant ministry when it's done with His model. To answer your other question: I think we practice humility, grace, and justice as Jesus did. It has nothing to do with the status quo, but everything to do with patience and grace. He did *not* think of Himself first, but became of no reputation, took the form of a servant, and loved and sacrificed. We can't count on people to be fair and noble and gracious, but we *can* work on our response to them and being the embodiment of grace. Good thoughts!

—Lisa

* * *

One thing I struggle with about Christian "humility" is that it's often not in sync with the way Jesus practiced humility. My best understanding is that humility means "an honest appraisal of oneself," so that it includes a healthy sense of self-respect as well as a profound understanding of our human weaknesses and tendency toward sinfulness. Now in the case of Jesus, I am not sure I understand what it meant for Him to be both Lord and man, but the way He practiced humility certainly wasn't to constantly acquiesce to injustice; in fact, He boldly stood against it. He risked and ultimately sacrificed His life not only because He was accused of blasphemy, but also because He threatened the status quo and the power structures of the Pharisees. Jesus kicked some serious table butt, because people of good faith were getting ripped off and spiritually gypped.

So like all spirituality, I don't think, based on Jesus' model, that there is a formula for practicing grace, justice, and humility. Sometimes it might mean dying on a cross or to ourselves; sometimes it might mean turning tables or being otherwise assertive and inappropriate for the sake of creating justice and removing oppression.

What are your thoughts?

—Jemila

* * *

Jemila,

Well, in regard to whether we should "turn over tables," I think Jesus did that both to fulfill prophecy and to "clean house"—His Father's house. I think He operated in perfection, which we don't do. We usually tie up our "rights" and "desires" and selfish ambitions to things we do. (If we're honest and can actually see it as that, of course.) I think it's hard to have righteous anger and not really sin, simply because we're bent with sinful nature. Yes, I think there are times to stand up for these things you speak of, especially guarding the weak—the elderly, the unborn, the disabled, the poor—but we have to know going into it that our ways are often not God's ways. It might turn out better if we take the path Jesus most often did. The turning-over-the-tables thing shouldn't overshadow the servanthood. I've noticed that people (not you) love that temple scene and love to mention it because it makes them feel justified. It also makes their emotions justified, which is okay, until we use them as a fortress. Have you noticed this? Every time one particular friend of mine gets upset and indignant, this passage surfaces. "Jesus had righteous anger," she says, but is my *friend's* anger really righteous? Is it consistently and persistently righteous? I feel skeptical about that. Is mine or yours? I wonder. Just something to think about. It's great to hear from you!

—Lisa

* * *

Hey Lisa,

I think you misunderstood the point of the metaphor of a seat at the table. The idea was that people who already have a seat reach out to those who do not—those who have been excluded, disenfranchised, and ignored—and invite them to join the feast. Your article seemed to assume the opposite, that it was about people who had no place at the table trying to force their way in.

I'd also try to be careful about painting with too broad a brush. Not everyone at the emerging women site fits your stereotype of the liberal mainliner. My own wife sure doesn't. In fact, you might want to be careful about throwing around words like *liberal* and *left*. In our postmodern, emerging context, those kinds of labels and dichotomies don't work so well anymore. The old Left-Right spectrum doesn't usually describe people's actual views anymore. At any rate, be careful of being so quick to label someone's views that you fail to actually hear what they're saying and consider if they might actually have a point.

Just some unsolicited advice.

—Mike

* * *

Mike,

Finally, a man weighs in! Hurrah. Thanks for all the advice. I guess I'm not sure about how to allude to someone with slightly more left-leaning political views than I, other than using quote marks. I did so to emphasize the point you made in your response.

My initial findings in the emergent conversation were left of center, but I have found other voices too. Thanks for clearing up the seat at the table confusion too; I didn't hear it put that way at www.emergingwomen .blogspot.com. I see it was a much different sort of gathering the way you put it.

I see you don't like labels. Yeah, me neither. I guess most people don't. It was almost like you were labeling me "quick to label," Mike. Or maybe "insensitive" or perhaps "misinformed." It's weird how that happens.

Thanks again!

TheOOZE is fun.

Peace out bro! Tell your wife, "Rock on Sister" for me.

—L

* * *

Just for perspective, I contribute fairly regularly to the emerging women blog. I generally vote Republican, don't hold any degrees beyond my bachelor's, am not ordained, am a stay-at-home mom, and probably qualify as more of a "nobody" than you. We would love to have you add your voice to our discussions if you'd like to level the playing field. There's not much we can do about who is taking part in the conversation other than to continue to make an open invitation.

I think maybe you should attend one of our conferences before making general statements about what it is we are trying to accomplish with them. (Reading that, it sounds more critical than I intended — it's so hard to convey tone in writing. I only mean that you would get a much better picture of what we want to accomplish and how we would like to see that done if you were with us in the flesh.) I attended the first of these last spring in Indiana at a little B&B, and it was *so* refreshing. I hope to be there for the Illinois one this year. Maybe we'll see you there?

—Cary

* * *

Thank you. It's great to hear from you and I greatly look forward to meeting you one day and attending a gathering of emerging women. That sounds wonderful. The adventure begins! I'm happy to even know there is one.

—Lisa

* * *

Lisa,

The reason it is right for women to ask for a place at the table is because there is a significant difference between humility and humiliation (as there is between submission and slavery). To be humble means to pass up a position of honor, to make yourself lower than you actually are. To be humiliated means to have your place at the table revoked not because you were presumptuous or prideful, but because you are a woman. You can see the distinction in the passage you cited: "'Give this man your seat.' Then, humiliated, you will have to take the least important place. But when you are invited, take the lowest place." Women have *not* been invited, and when a man comes along, frequently women are told, "Give this man your seat, because he is a man and you aren't."

Of course, how we behave at the table should be appropriate to our place as members of the community, children of the Father, persons in the process of becoming like Jesus. And yes, more humility is in order in these conversations (I include myself in this calling for more humility and gracious listening). But I will not be content to just pick up crumbs under the table unless that is where I have chosen to sit, not been forced to sit by the males at the table. Because I believe that Jesus (and Paul) invited and included women in conversation, relationship, and ministry in a radically inclusive way (for their time in history) and the efforts to keep women in their place (even by women themselves) are to reject the freedom that Jesus died to call us into. It is not up to us to make a space for ourselves, He has done that. Others have denied women (along with other "outsiders") their place in the kingdom, not the Lord. Just as Jesus defended Mary from her sister's condemnation, I believe it is our place to sit at *His* feet—but at *His* feet alongside our brothers—not at our brothers' feet, unless that is where we choose to serve. As free persons, not as slaves.

Peace, Adriene

* * *

Interesting thoughts. Thank you.

Your comments were insightful and to me they emphasize even more the sacrifice of Jesus. He was humiliated willingly for us. He was made our shame. He became our sin. He was willing to die naked and publicly for people who hated Him. And for people who may never be humble or willing to be humiliated.

—Lisa

* * *

Lisa,

I've gotten some good insights and conviction from your article in terms of asking God for a spirit of humility, being open to the Spirit and focusing on being faithful to a calling rather than being antsy for recognition or seeking self-promotion inappropriately out of insecurity or whatever. I know it's tough receiving criticism too, and you've gotten quite a bit for what you wrote, which was out of the genuineness of your heart. But in your last post, I really felt you lost your witness and credibility. You came across as self-righteous, superior, and condemning. And spiritually manipulative and abusive. I feel that you owe Adriene a significant and heartfelt apology.

I would also add that Jesus had a specific calling to bear humiliation for a higher purpose—sometimes we might too, but humiliation for its own sake is not godly; for God affirms the dignity and value of every human being and invites each of us to the table. So generalizing that all women should accept humiliation and degradation for all other women as part of following Jesus just doesn't make sense. That's like condoning slavery, rather than working creatively to change the individuals and societies that perpetuate it.

—Rainy

* * *

Rainy,

I certainly didn't want to come across as all those terrible things you've accused me of. I think you interpreted my comments as judging, instead of as my reflections on what God has done for me. Adriene just inspired those reflections by her comment.

—Lisa

＊　＊　＊

Hi. I resonate with your thoughts. Insider/outsider distinctions are real and the perception of whether someone is truly welcome or not is a major issue in Christian community. Do I fit here? Am I one of the community or is there something I must change/do/be/prove before I should be here? I went to the Round Barn gathering of emerging women, and met wonderful women who were in various areas of work. Ministry, church planting, partner of a church planter, writing, women who are not quite sure women should be pastors, women who take for granted we are to be pastors, boundary-breaking women, women who don't realize it but they are boundary-making. Emergent has boundaries and has diversity within. So who is really welcome? I am one of those liberal, ordained, PhD, MDiv, and all that you mentioned, but I don't take any offense at the comments! Nothing of a degree or position or responsibilities in the Christian community makes me feel any more or less emergent. But I do relate to your seat-at-the-table issue. It didn't really seem I was more welcome because of my various statuses. . . . I'm not sure really what makes one feel inside, welcomed, at the table in emergent. What do you think? In church terms, what is the process of welcoming in emergent? Openness of blogs—that's welcoming. Reciprocated communication, open invitations to events, mutual respect, each party able to present an authentic self without fear of harm or censure, enjoying people both because of the differences and because of the similarities. We are all on a faith journey. Thank you for your thoughtful challenge to be more Christlike in our ways, and humble in our manners!

—Karen

* * *

Rev. Karen,

Really nice to hear your comments. I'm glad an ordained woman weighed in. I really respect the study you've done on your spiritual journey. Even more, I respect your humble attitude, and not putting yourself on any pedestal. This is grace in action. I'm considering getting my MA in religion next fall with a concentration in spiritual formation at EST to better inform my writing and speaking. I love education, especially if it makes me fall in love with my Creator more.

It's been more than two months since I submitted the article here to TheOOZE, and since then I have gotten a much better feel for the conversation, and indeed, felt more at home. I think sometimes we don't feel welcome when we don't feel represented. It is as if there is an unspoken norm that keeps certain types out. This can be real or imagined. In my emergent experience, at this point, it is far more imagined than real.

A conscious effort to reach out to other vantage points and perspectives guarantees a more fruitful exchange of ideas, and fosters creativity to engage the challenges of our postmodern culture, in my opinion. As we are mindful to have a humble, Christlike walk, and bear spiritual fruit in our lives, I think we can more fully serve the kingdom. Overall, I hope my article spawned more thoughtful contemplation than discord, and more Spirit-driven conviction to be more like Jesus, our Savior, than to be like anyone else, including our old selves.

—Lisa

JACKSON, GOD, AND ME

A Meditation Before Jackson Pollock's *Autumn Rhythm* (Number 30)

MURRAY RICHMOND / AUGUST 16, 2005

It is a warm, beautiful November day in New York City, and I should be outside basking in the sun because my plane leaves for Fairbanks, Alaska, in eight hours. Instead, I am sitting on a tan bench inside the Metropolitan Museum of Art, struggling to see the painting in front of me.

I am not trying to understand the painting. I am not trying to find any hidden meanings in it. I am not even trying to enjoy it. As a matter of fact, I am trying pretty hard not to do those things. I am just trying to see it for what it is — a painting. Of course my mind rebels against the simplicity of this task, and this feels like some of the hardest work I have done in weeks — harder than writing a sermon, which is where I usually exert this kind of effort.

The painting holding this hook in me is Jackson Pollock's *Autumn Rhythm* (Number 30), a swirl of colors he flung onto the canvas in his Long Island studio. It is a huge holy mess of ordered chaos, a cacophony of fall colors. The splatters and trails of black, gray, brown, and white paint thrown onto the canvas create an initial sense of visual dissonance, not rhythm as the title suggests. It is a secular creation of frenzied beauty.

I am not well versed in modern art, but I know that if I am going to see it — really see it — I have to enter into the chaos of this creation, resisting any temptation to provide order where there is none, to insert some kind of hip understanding where there is nothing to be understood. I have to experience the painting, not conquer it with my intellect.

Autumn Rhythm (Number 30) has no center, no pattern, no discernible borders, and it tells no story. It is not a "religious" painting by any stretch of the imagination, but I am sitting here because I am sure that if God is like anything I know on earth, the Most Holy One is like this painting.

"There was a reviewer," Pollock said, "who wrote that my pictures didn't have a beginning or an end. He didn't mean it as a compliment, but it was. It was a fine compliment." That is just a mere metaphysical step away from eternity—Alpha and Omega.

This is not a religious painting, but I find it more compelling than most contemporary "Christian" art I see plastered in religious bookstores. Most of that is poorly done propaganda—pictures of Jesus the hero, saving the drug addict, hovering over the crib, descending into the world with cheap vestiges of glory. These pictures are trying too hard to be holy and to convert me, and they fail miserably at both.

But *Autumn Rhythm* (Number 30) feels like holy primordial stuff of the pre-Creation. It does not capture a moment in time, it is a moment frozen in a time. The painting corresponds to nothing in nature, and yet the painting is, and the moment the painting captures is an eternal moment.

I try hard not to think about these things. I shake them off and go back to my attempts at just looking at *Autumn Rhythm* (Number 30). Pollock's paint-splattered canvas is everything we want to believe that the world is not—undisciplined, chaotic, frenzied, and devoid of any fixed point. It is sensuous, but without sensibility.

Ancient mystical theologians such as Pseudo-Dionysus and the anonymous author of *The Cloud of Unknowing* tell me I can only hear the voice of God if I can set aside all preconceptions of God, and just let the great I AM simply be. They have always understood that God is best perceived through apophasis—the way of the divine darkness, the way of ignorance, the way of the desert. We can only see the Light by entering the darkness. We only hear the Voice by entering into the silence. We can only experience the fullness of God by entering the void.

I cannot really experience God through my knowledge or my reason, because then I am really only experiencing my own limited knowledge of God, my own limited understanding of God. Facts about God fill my head and leave little room for the Eternal Voice. A head full of knowledge about God does not lead me to knowledge of God.

This all feels faintly heretical, but I recently found an unlikely ally in the apostle Paul, that cocksure convert, who writes to the Corinthian church, "Anyone who claims to know something does not yet have the necessary knowledge" (1 Corinthians 8:2, NRSV). He said this in the context of trying to resolve a church fight, where one party was trying to prove they knew God better than the other. "If you think you know too much," Paul says, "You end up knowing nothing of importance." Knowledge is not the ultimate trump card.

Autumn Rhythm forces me to unknow all I know about painting. Like the creative voice of God roaring out of the chaos, Pollock's work refuses to be stuck in a quaint category, it refuses to be indicative of something, it refuses to stand in stead for something greater than itself. It just is.

By the time Pollock painted this he had given up any hope that art could be representative of reality. Art was its own reality, and spoke with its own voice. Rather than painting pictures of things, Pollock wanted the painting to be the thing itself. This canvas does not mean anything, does not say anything, does not represent anything. I must take it on its own terms, for it offers nothing else.

Maybe if I can unknow God, I can find truth. Maybe by giving myself swirling chaos, I can find the ultimate order of God. Maybe if I can approach the emptiness of silence, I can finally learn to speak of the fullness of God.

At the end of his *Tractatus Logico-Philosophicus*, Ludwig Wittgenstein said, "What we cannot speak about we must pass over in silence." *Autumn*

Rhythm (Number 30) reduces me to silence. It stands totally out of context with the world I know. By making no statement, by seeking no reference to the world around it, by merely existing, it inadvertently brings me face to face with the God who is I AM. This painting demands a new language, an unspoken language that consists only of the spaces between words. If only I could experience God as I am experiencing this painting.

If only I could preach the silence this painting is birthing in me.

Of course, as a preacher, I do not have the option of silence. I am a purveyor of words, and I doubt my congregation would appreciate a steady diet of silent sermons, even if they do make constant jokes about the length of the ones I do give.

But at heart I know that *Autumn Rhythm* is analogous to true preaching.

I usually rise at five on Sunday mornings to write my sermons. The world is very quiet then, especially in the dead of the Alaskan winter. I meditate all week on the text, on the outline of my message, on illustrations and stories I can use. But I can rarely commit myself to the actual words I will preach until I am forced to. When I first started preaching, I would finish writing my sermons on Wednesdays. (When I told that to an incredulous colleague of mine, he said, "Well then, what do you do during the offertory?") These days it is usually — almost always — only the urgency of the deadline that motivates me.

I have been preaching for fifteen years, and people tell me I am pretty good at it. But each Sunday makes me feel like I know less and less about what I am really doing.

Each Sunday I feel like I am only diminishing God with my words. But sometimes preaching works — more often than I want to admit.

In Steven Naifeh and Gregory White Smith's massive biography *Jackson Pollock: An American Saga*, one eyewitness to Pollock's technique says that he would "take his stick or brush out of the paint can and then, in a cursive sweep, pass it over the canvas high above, so that the viscous paint would form trailing patterns which hover over the canvas before they settle upon it, and then fall into it, and then leave a trace of their own passage. He is not drawing on the canvas so much as the air above it."[1]

Pollock called his painting "memories arrested in space." His paintings are merely the residue of a dance of paint that once swirled above the canvas.

Perhaps that is the best way to understand the preaching—to find the Word in between the words. When I preach, I fling words in the air; I toss empty verbal symbols of God over the heads of my parishioners. But these words are somehow inspired by God, by the Scriptures, by my experiences with God, and by my experiences with God's people. They dance in the air around the people who hear them and fall on ears that are receptive to the dance.

I never know how people are going to react to a sermon. Sometimes I think I have written a masterpiece, only to watch people nod with dull acceptance as I inflict my "genius" on them.

I remember the worst sermon I ever gave. I struggled all week trying to write it, but nothing came. When Sunday morning worship rolled around I had to say something—so I splattered enough words on the pages to show that I had not spent the week playing computer games. The sermon was a rambling wreck of poorly written slipshod ideas, and I was so ashamed of it that I sped through it as fast as I could, praying I could find a merciful ending. But after the service one woman, a stranger to me, sought me out, held my hands with her trembling hands, and through her tears uttered a soft, "Thank you."

As much as I would like to think she was thanking me for finally ending the sermon, I know that somehow my homiletic disaster ushered her into the healing presence of God.

A sermon "captures" the essence of God about as much as Pollock's canvases captured the dance of paint that once hovered over them. If we don't see the dance of God in the words, if we only hear the words that are the residue of that dance, the sermon will be but a cold witness to a long-gone event. But if somehow we can join the dance, then the Word becomes alive for us as well in the preaching.

Pollock's work reminds me that I cannot "capture" the essence of God with my own words. If I am really good, I may point to the God of the still point, but I must always remember Vladimir Lossky's words: "If in seeing God one can know what one sees, then one has not seen God in Himself but something intelligible, something which is inferior to Him. It is by unknowing that one may know Him who is above every possible object of knowledge."[2] Just as I must take *Autumn Rhythm* on its own terms and let it simply be the painting it is, so must I approach God on God's own terms, letting God be who God is. My words cannot capture God, but they may be captured by the presence of God, and then, and only then will they be useful.

I speak too much, and anyone who knows me will confirm that with a powerful "Amen!" My words have few deep spaces between them and are cheapened with overuse. I try too hard to be "meaningful" and "deep." I am guilty of that even as I write this sentence.

So I go to *Autumn Rhythm*, which doesn't say anything. It just is. Maybe it will teach me something. It is not trying to sell me anything, it is not trying to convert me to anything, it is not trying to teach me anything, and it certainly is not preaching to me. It is in no way practical. It just is.

It is not trying to point me to God, and for that very reason, it does.

So I sit here, on this tan bench, staring. Other spectators file by, noting that this is a famous painting by a famous painter, and then they move to the next famous painting. I sit and stare and try to see the painting. A school group gathers around the painting, and the girls giggle with each other while the boys try to look cool by looking bored. And still I stare, working hard not to work hard at seeing it. I make descriptive notes in a black notebook I bought at the museum store. Some people are staring at me rather than the painting, but still I stare, trying to see it in my soul, trying to let it enter me, trying to not appreciate it, to not understand it — just to see it. One gregarious soul asks me what the painting is about, and I tell him I do not know.

THOMAS M. RICHMOND III is the pastor of the University Community Presbyterian Church in Fairbanks, Alaska.

WONDERING

I MENTIONED EARLIER HOW MUCH I love being a dad. One of the greatest things about it is getting to watch my children at play. My daughter Gracie is five now, and she loves to dance. Sometimes we'll have big family dance parties where everyone gets in on the action. Gracie loves trying out new dance moves and watching her shadow on the curtains. Other times she'll want to have singing contests with us while we're out in public. "Here, Daddy, your turn," she'll say, handing the imaginary microphone to me in the middle of Carl's Jr.

My son Alden is nine now, and lately I've noticed he's not dancing quite as much these days.

"Alden, why aren't you dancing?" I asked him one night.

"I'm not very good, Dad," came the reply.

"What?" I questioned him. "You're a great dancer. You used to dance with us all the time."

"No, I'm not very good."

I'm not sure what happened, but somewhere along the way Alden lost some of his childlike wonder and confidence. It happens to all of us eventually, I guess. People tell us we can't, and we believe them.

Then there are all the rules we learn along the way. Good church-going people don't do this, or you can't do this or that in church. You can't think about God that way. You can't worship like that.

Over time, we stop asking "why" or "what if" or "why not." Often we settle into a life of resignation, or as John Eldredge and Brent Curtis write in *The Sacred Romance*, we "hunker down and make life work here and now."

In this next section, you'll see people challenging that thinking and daring once again to ask "what if." They're giving themselves permission to go outside the bounds of traditional thinking about church—if even for a moment—and endeavor to find a new way forward.

When I was pastoring, I'd often have people come to me and confide that they felt burned out and dry in their spiritual lives. So I'd ask them what they were doing when they felt that way. If it was devotions, I'd tell them stop doing devotions for a while. If it was acts of service, I'd tell them to stop serving others for a while.

Whatever it was that they were doing to try to get close to God, I'd tell them to do exactly the opposite.

The weird thing is that it worked. Sometimes they returned to those expressions after they took a break and sometimes they didn't. Sometimes they found new ways of communing with God. But it was the breaking away, the giving oneself permission that ultimately led to breakthrough.

The authors in this section are not necessarily looking for agreement, but rather an awareness of the issues and the growing breadth and depth of the conversations.

SUSPICION AND SISTERHOOD

A Brief Theoretical Meditation

NATHAN P. GILMOUR / APRIL 6, 2006

You know how those fundamentalists are. Don't you? Perhaps the suspicion entered my own mind when I entered real friendships with self-named fundamentalists. As I held conversations, this possibility occurred to me: What they're saying isn't nonsense; it has a logic to it. But its content still strikes me as wrong. Not content to dismiss this sensation nor to assume that all difference leads inevitably to relativistic "equality," I began to realize that until these conversations, I'd been applying a hermeneutic of suspicion to fundamentalists.

By "hermeneutic of suspicion" I mean an approach to one's neighbor that assumes the neighbor's dishonesty, whether because of subconscious repression or class-numbed conscience or just plain meanness. If you think you see virtue, you scrape at it, hoping to find corruption or power hunger or allegiance to unworthy allies and masters. There's no real need to ask a writer why she or he writes what she or he writes; the answer is right there in the text, or more likely in the catch phrases. When a Calvinist says "sovereignty" he really means "hatred." When a Catholic mentions "community" she really means "control." And so on.

It's a fairly common way of reading texts in university literature classes and under its banner the art of literary criticism (or at least sectors of it) has become a game in which the critic proves her or his superiority to the author at hand. The critic isn't as misogynistic as Milton, not as self-deluded as Wordsworth, not as imperialistic as Dante. In church life it's even more stifling: whenever anyone, within or outside my tradition, says or does things differently, my own suspicion, not my neighbor's rationale, determines what the ritual or teaching means. Usually she or he is out to destroy something important: The Protestant thinks himself a little god, irrespective of proper authority. The charismatic thinks she's holier and more spiritual than me. The liberal holds me in contempt, thinking me parochial and ignorant.

The hermeneutic is not hard to spot. A writer might begin sentences with "although," use verbs of appearance like *looks* or *seems*, and finish sentences with "really" clauses: "Although they might seem to be concerned about people's eternities, the reality is that they're only after money." Everything, directly or indirectly, is at root driven by the opponent's two or three main vices. "Their thirst for power is obviously behind their claims to exclusive truth." See? It's not hard to write either.

The hermeneutic of suspicion assumes that one's conversation partner, be that partner a book or a person, is an enemy and that the proper response to an enemy is to avoid being taken. And sometimes such a stance is necessary. Some people genuinely are enemies. But not everybody is, and therein lies the difficulty with the hermeneutic of suspicion.

As a more edifying alternative, I propose a hermeneutic of rehearsal. I've borrowed it mostly from Alasdair MacIntyre's *After Virtue*. Instead of picking up on offending bits and rhetorically awkward catch phrases, we Christians could instead take the other person's thought as a whole, patiently reflecting on what she or he has to say. The rehearsal name comes from the test of that reflection: If I can rehearse your position to your satisfaction, so that you can say to me when I'm done, "Yes, that's basically what I meant," then we can undertake the project of critiquing the idea or system together. Such would be the defining intellectual practice, the starting point for Christian intellectual inquiry.

So systems of thought are not invulnerable in this paradigm, but instead of lining up as armies to defend this or that way of thinking, we engage them together, understanding them first and then discerning whether their value, as tools or as frameworks or as whatever metaphor we set up to evaluate them, outweighs the harm that they might do. Ideas mean something, and through the Spirit's guidance with a little help from the saints from across the centuries and around the globe, we Christians can at least tentatively say that this system is better for this purpose and for these reasons. We needn't relapse into relativism nor assert more loudly than our neighbor; instead of "your" ideas clashing with "mine," we work with "ours" with the goal of building up our neighbors and the church and our witness to the gospel of Jesus the Messiah.

NATHAN D. GILMOUR teaches writing, literature, philosophy, and biblical studies (all inside the English department) as he finishes his PhD in English. He also serves his congregation as Minister of Education and, most importantly, lives as husband to Mary and father to Micah.

CHURCH RESTRUCTURE

ALAN HARTUNG / DECEMBER 27, 2006

Seated in a sanctuary with twelve hundred other persons, I listened to the associate pastor announce a great need for workers. Small group leaders, children's church helpers, Sunday School teachers, you name it, they needed it. It was about that time I first heard the principle that 80 percent of the church will not do any of the work, while 20 percent do all of the work. That was nearly a decade ago, and since that time, I have heard the 80-20 principle time and time again.

Church growth experts may tell you the proper response to this principle is to spend 80 percent of your time with the 20 percent who are doing the work. Or possibly they will suggest ways to network with the 80 percent, so you can increase the percentage of people who are laboring in the church. Almost all advice centers on the idea that slight modifications within current structures or changes in emphases will improve results.

But what if the 80-20 principle actually results from the structure itself? Current church structures are designed for large numbers of people to merely attend church. The myriad of working positions currently available in most churches would not be necessary without the large numbers of people who have no other responsibility beyond that of showing up.

This principle will hold true as long as the Sunday worship service, in its current form, is the center of church life. The Sunday service is geared around worship, possibly communion, and the sermon. At a bare minimum, you need a worship team (or a leader who can play guitar), a preacher, and child-care workers. Of course, persons to prepare the bulletin, change the lyrics on the overhead, clean the sanctuary (and bathrooms), and to usher would also be necessary. Greeters at the door are always nice, but maybe the ushers could double up on that duty. Recruiting the number of people it takes to pull off a quality Sunday service can seem like a never-ending battle.

Most—if not all—of these jobs hold one thing in common: they are not necessary unless you have a crowd of people coming who do not do any of these things. In its current form, the Sunday worship service creates a need for large numbers of nonworkers. The 80-20 principle should be the expected result when the Sunday worship service is the central focus of the church—the design dictates it.

A pastoral staff could choose to just accept the principle as the way of life for the church. Perhaps, in our culture, it is the best way to introduce people to the church. After they have been introduced to the church, you can try to transition them into some sort of ministry position (this is probably the heart of the seeker-sensitive model).

Another option not often looked at is to shift the focus of a church. This is not a simple thing. One church I know of has begun using small group rhetoric in an attempt to get the focus off of the Sunday service: "We are no longer a church with small groups. We are a small group church." To date, only about twenty percent of the members of that church are involved in a small group.

Some churches have had greater success than that, but few churches dedicate the required resources to successfully make such a shift. Rhetoric and even a good number of people dedicated to small groups is not enough to truly shift the focus off the Sunday worship service. As long as the bulk of church resources are consumed by the Sunday service, it will be the focus of your church. And with that focus, the 80-20 principle will apply.

A shifting of resources significant enough to change the focus requires tremendous sacrifice. Before a staff, eldership, board, or congregation pursues such a step, the costs must be counted. To start, many persons in the 80 percent group enjoy being in the 80 percent group. They simply like having no responsibility. Also, with the current format engrained in the evangelical psyche, any changes will feel awkward—even for those recognizing the need for the change. Additionally, a shift in church models will most likely make it difficult on paid staff; the lines will be significantly blurred between who should be paid for their services and who should not be paid.

In addition to these things, the definition of success must be radically redefined. When success is defined as numerical growth, the pressure to draw a crowd will beat down any attempt to shift the focus of the church. For the church plant I am working with, the definition of success is developing a community which embodies life in the kingdom of God. This has been our definition of success from the beginning, yet we still struggle with the idea that numerical growth is the standard of measure in American Evangelicalism.

After careful evaluation, if a church still wants to shift the focus, a new model must be chosen. Above, I mentioned small groups as the possible focus (this means more than just having small groups in your church). I do not consider it the best option, but presently it is the most common choice. Other possibilities include: planting new and smaller churches, dividing the congregation, or starting ministries which may be called "church within a church." Changing the entire format of a Sunday worship service to reflect different values is another option. Whatever model a church pursues, the structure should not work against the goals, as the current model does.

Once a model is chosen, the difficult task of shifting the resources of the church must take place. By resources, I mean everything the church has at its disposal: people, funds, property, etc. If most of the finances and laborers in the church are dedicated to the Sunday service, the resources have not been shifted enough. There is no formula to determine how much of a shift needs to take place; each church will have its own unique problems and solutions.

If a sufficient number of persons is not devoted to the change, division will surely follow. Change is always painful, and unfortunately, some will choose not to endure the pain. If the leadership of the church is convinced the 80-20 principle is neither healthy nor biblical, changing the structure is inevitable. Consequently, the loss of some of the 80 percent group is also inevitable. And don't be surprised if some of the 20 percent group bail on you as well (some in this group love being in the minority group of "committed" members).

Specific changes from this point are highly contextual to the model a church has chosen to pursue. Changes are difficult for people, and care should be taken not to do too much, too fast. Changing too slowly, however, could be a sign that the fear of the costs is greater than the desire to change.

Given the high costs of change, few will engage in this journey. Those who decide to pursue this change must tread carefully. A deep-seated belief that people are harmed by a model or the church is falling short because of the model will be necessary to weather the storm. Of course, if a conviction that strong is held, not making the changes would be a violation of conscience.

ALAN HARTUNG is the general editor of TheOOZE, a podcaster ("A Different Perspective"), and an actor. And, just because he thinks he is not busy enough, he does freelance webdesign, website hosting, and domain sales (www.SoCalWebsites.com), since his other "jobs" really don't pay (except for the occasional acting gig!).

LEADING FROM THE MARGINS, PART VI

Mystics, Poets, and Dreamers

LEN HJALMARSON / DECEMBER 9, 2005

Christopher Alexander is an architect who advocates building in process and not from a plan. He argues that this is the ancient way, and that the modern and mechanistic approach demonstrates our lack of spirituality.

Alexander relates that one of the fundamental problems in architecture arises when the building is going up and the designer must make simple choices. For example, should this column be five or six inches in diameter? He talked about how the designer's own ego could get in the way of constructing the right building. The question he would finally ask is: "Which choice is a greater gift to God?" He continued: "You can build a building that everyone says is wonderful—a success—but does that make it wonderful or a success? No. You can build a building that no one says is wonderful or a success. But can it be wonderful and a success? Yes."[1]

When we reduce truth to formulas or success to size, we are far along the road of idolatry and the worship of technique. We have sold out to the evil empire, and forgotten that we are strangers and aliens here. Walter Brueggemann has continued to remind us that we are in fact living in times that parallel the exile. In *Finally Comes the Poet*, he calls us to a new kind of speech to square off against the reductionism of the age: "To address the issue of truth greatly reduced requires us to be poets who speak against the prose world. . . . Poetic speech is the only proclamation worth doing in a situation of reductionism. . . . This offer requires special care for words, because the baptized community awaits speech in order to be a faithful people."[2]

Around the time of Constantine, the church, which had lived in the heart of its people, passed control to managers, most of whom were lackeys of the empire. It became dangerous to talk about beauty or write poetry after this time, because beauty and poetry can inspire dreams of a different world. The rulers of the age knew what the poets had long understood: The pen is mightier than the sword, and a simple idea can inspire revolution.

> All people dream, but not equally.
> Those who dream by night,
> in the dusty recesses of their minds,
> wake in the day to find that it was vanity.
> But the dreamers of the day are dangerous,
> for they may act their dreams with open eyes
> to make it possible. [3]

Since that time the mainstream of Christendom has been dominated by managers, while the mystics have been marginalized. Consider this quote, often attributed to a Chinese businessman traveling in the U.S.: "When I meet a Buddhist monk, I meet a holy man. When I meet a Christian pastor, I meet a manager."

Occasionally, mystics become managers, giving in to the temptations of power. At other times managers arise who are also mystics. Some of these dreamers are marginalized, but some leave their mark on the church by bringing renewal to an old wineskin, or by founding new movements (like Menno Simons, Zinzendorf, Wesley, or Wimber). Others are marginalized and embrace it, caring for those around them and transforming their own small corners of society with the love and grace of Jesus. Some of these marginalized dreamers find themselves with followers, and in turn birth movements of renewal that recover lost components of the gospel, like St. Francis and his brothers.

Alan Roxburgh, author of *The Sky Is Falling*, writes, "Poets make available a future that does not exist as yet; they are eschatologically oriented. From this environment, a missional imagination emerges."[4] In the past, disenfranchised poets and priests had little option but to remain on the margins, voices speaking in the silence, alone and without influence. But times have changed.

With the prominence of the Internet, websites like Ginkworld and TheOOZE, networks like ALLELON, a multiplicity of forums, and magazines like *Reality*, *Relevant*, and *Next Wave*, we have virtual watering holes where once was desert. Conversations spring up like mushrooms, and conversations are the fabric of community life. Dreamers and marginalized leaders meet and encourage one another. New ways of being are imagined and performed. Many of these dreamers are involved in innovative efforts that are impacting their neighbors with the gospel, and their combined voices are more than a chorus calling for change; by their example, they inspire it.

- "If we dream alone, it remains merely a dream. If many dream together, then it is the beginning of a new reality."[5]
- "It is this capacity to articulate a preferred future based on a common moral vision that allows people to dream again."[6]

One of the core tasks of leadership is to help the community to dream again. In order to dream together we must be connected. Fritjof Capra, quoting Margaret Wheatley, remarks that "facilitating emergence means first building up and nurturing networks of communication in order to 'connect the system to more of itself.'"[7] The power of new media to facilitate feedback loops contributes to emergence. Just as a new medium empowered the first reformation, new media are empowering a second reformation.

THE NEED FOR MENTORS

We desperately need a new kind of Christian, one who is self-authorizing and looks to Jesus and not to human authority as she moves forward as an apprentice, obedient to a heavenly vision. Too many gifted people are waiting for permission from leaders who have a vested interest in things staying as they are. They won't give it. We need to model and teach that "His anointing teaches you about all things. . . . Abide in Him" (1 John 2:27, NASB).

At the same time, we need mentors. The role of mentors is to point searchers to God, and encourage their dependence on Him. The role of mentors is to show by example how to walk forward without certainty, but with faith and hope and love. The role of mentors is to lift others up, to serve without consideration of recognition or reward. If we can model this kind of service, we will help to birth a new kind of leader by our example.

Alan Roxburgh argues that the communities we need will be led by an abbot or abbess:

> The Abbot's role is to guard the ethos. He/she is continually asking: 'Are we living the story? Are we keeping the ethos?' Abbots live the ethos among others and in so doing are saying, 'This is what we do as members of the Order; it may also be what you want to do.' Therefore, the Abbot's role is deeply relational and interpretive, continually inviting others into exploration not program.
> Today we have lots of Apostle figures but few Abbots.[8]

Lasting change will spring up within communities that exist for something larger than themselves. Leaders must empower that change so that the margins become our new center.

LEN HJALMARSON and his family live in the fruitful Okanagan region of British Columbia. Len is a writer and dreamer and sometimes wishes he had been born a *pomme couteur* or vintner. Len is currently a student in the DMN program at ACTS Seminaries in Langley, BC, and spends his days designing software for combat simulations. In his quieter moments, he enjoys pruning apple trees, canoeing down a lazy river, or thinking of ways to improve a fruit cake recipe. Check out his blog, NextReformation.com. This article is one of a seven-part series. Read the complete series at TheOOZE.com.

NO COUNTRY FOR OLD MEN

DOUG JACKSON / DECEMBER 12, 2002

John O'Keefe, in an otherwise excellent article entitled "Image or Imagery," describes his ideal emergent congregation. In addition to a killer website and coffee-house seating, he notes, "Best of all, the only blue hair in the place was on the tips of the worship leader's spikes." I hear and read a great deal about the inclusive nature of the postmodern worldview, but the "only" in John's sentence makes me nervous.

The modern church demanded uniformity and more or less tolerated the young as they followed their dyspeptic path through the denominational digestive system, eventually emerging as fully conformed grownups with short haircuts and dark suits. Hardened nonconformists were simply excreted. I fully acknowledge the justice of Leonard Sweet's remark, "We like one type of blue hairs (60+), but not another (30-)." As the old cliche has it, however, the oppressed make the worst oppressors, and I believe the worst thing that could happen is that people could truthfully say of the postmodern church what Yeats, in "Sailing to Byzantium," said of western modernity: "That is no country for old men." In fact, given the worship style generally associated with azure mohawks, we might include the later lines, "Caught in that sensual music all neglect / Monuments of unageing intellect." Or, to put it more succinctly, Leviticus 19:32 still applies.

Does postmodernism require that we write off the elderly, or would postmodern inclusivism demand that we embrace them? In fact, I would argue that a strong feature of modernism, with its obsession with efficiency and product, was a rejection of old age. By contrast, ancient cultures embraced age as a sign of wisdom: one was no longer valued for what one could do, but for what one knew. I am aware it creates some real train wrecks with the whole worship style thing (as an ex-modern pre-postmodern pastor, believe me, I know all about the balancing act!), but again, isn't the genius of postmodernism its willingness to wrestle with community instead of seeking the good of the largest constituency? Or will we simply agree, to return to Yeats, that "An aged man is but a paltry thing / A ragged coat upon a stick"?

Two stories might help move us forward.

The first story concerns the fact that my home state of Texas is considering rescinding the fifteen dollar bounty on coyotes. The government originally offered this blood money on the premise that these varmints had overpopulated, leading to predations on the stock of ranchers, encroachments on urban areas, and the spread of disease. Recent findings, however, indicate that the bounty might be the cause, rather than the cure, of such problems. The theory runs, in part, like this: Hunters tend to kill adult males as the most visible target. This leaves the pups with no one to train them in the intricate skill of hunting wild game. As a result, they gravitate to the easy pickings created by human habitation: calves, sheep, domestic pets, and the contents of garbage cans. Result: more coyotes with greater dependence on humans. To paraphrase Yeats, when the panhandle becomes no country for old coyotes, the adolescents make trouble for themselves and everybody else.

The second story comes from my own congregation. Bob and Betty, an elderly couple in our church, have been married for more than fifty years. A few years ago, Betty went suddenly blind from macular degeneration. That summer, our senior adults took a trip to Branson, Missouri, where no doubt they listened to music many of us would not tolerate at gunpoint. They returned late on a Sunday afternoon, planning, because they are senior adults, simply to disembark from the bus and go straight to evening worship. (Skipping church was not, of course, an option.) A few minutes after they arrived, several of us were standing in the sanctuary when one of our men, a classic example of an arrested-development Boomer, wandered in with an awestruck look on his face. "Do you know what I just saw?" he asked us. "Bob is in the fellowship hall painting Betty's fingernails. They don't have time to go home, but she doesn't want to come into church not looking her best. She can't see to do it herself, so he's in there painting her fingernails."

I've told that story from the pulpit more than once. Just the other day, on his website, my sixteen-year-old son (who wears black T-shirts, combat boots, and jeans decorated with Officer Negative patches, and does not have blue hair only because my wife and I had to draw the line somewhere) was posting his replies to one of those online surveys. To the question, "What do you want to be when you grow up?" he responded, "I want to be an old man who paints his wife's fingernails because she's too blind to do it herself and doesn't want to go to church not looking her best."

Both as parent and pastor, I would tolerate any amount of organ music to purchase that lesson for our youth.

Yeats' narrator, frustrated in his search for a mentor in the modern west, announces, "And therefore I have sailed the seas and come / To the holy city of Byzantium." That line, combined with the ageism we see in much postmodern praxis, might go a long way to explain the sudden resurgence of Greek Orthodox Christianity: People really are sailing to Byzantium. If those of us in the free-church tradition wish to be true to our postmodern propaganda (to say nothing of our Bibles and our teenagers), we must find a way to pray, again, with Yeats' narrator:

> O sages standing in God's holy fire
> As in the gold mosaic of a wall,
> Come from the holy fire, perne in a gyre,
> And be the singing-masters of my soul.

DoUg JAcKSoN is a former football player and wrestler, a current husband and father, and a sometimes writer. After twenty-three years as a pastor, Doug went over the wall and is now director of Logsdon Seminary programs and congregational resourcing at the South Texas School of Christian Studies in Corpus Christi, Texas.

GOD-PLEASING EVANGELISM

GREGORY JENSEN / DECEMBER 24, 2004

For Christians it is certainly easier, and frankly more comforting, to assume that people do not accept the gospel because of their own pride, indifference, or lack of faith. And while in some cases this may be true, it is an explanation which too easily allows those of us who are Christians to avoid our own responsibility in other people's rejection of Christ.

Often gospel presentations seem calculated to force (either intellectually or emotionally) a person to accept Christ. Someone's well-meaning, if not clumsy, attempt at doing good, amounts to coercion. Sometimes this evangelism even reflects a desire to control others or to glorify oneself.

Whatever the reason, however, any hint of coercion or manipulation violates the gospel. The standard for Christian outreach and evangelism must be Christ himself, who, in the words of the Russian Orthodox lay theologian Pavel Evdokimov, had an "incomprehensible respect for [human] freedom."

This incomprehensible divine respect for human freedom lies at the center of the gospel. Think for a moment about the Christ's conception. God doesn't manipulate the virgin Mary or (worse still to imagine) force himself on her. No, God sends the archangel Gabriel, his best man, if you will, to invite Mary to receive Christ into her life, into her body. And once the invitation has been extended, God waits for her consent. It is as if God, the angels, and the whole creation hold their collective breath and wait in silent expectation for the consent of this young girl. Then, from the depth of her heart, freely and without reservations, Mary consents to God's invitation and sings out: "Behold the handmaid of the Lord: be it unto me according to thy word" (Luke 1:38, KJV). There was on God's part no force, no manipulation or coercion; He simply made an offer with respect and consideration for Mary's freedom and dignity.

God-pleasing, to say nothing of effective, evangelism begins with an imitation of the respect God extends to each human person. If we are to be faithful imitators of Christ, we must avoid any violation of human freedom and dignity. "We must avoid," as Evdokimov tells us, "any compelling proof [that] violates human conscience [and] changes faith into mere knowledge."

Even as I write these words I can hear the objections: Christ proclaimed the kingdom of God with power and authority, with signs and wonders, with miraculous cures and deliverance from demons! While not wishing to deny God's miracles, or the need for Christian preaching, I think we too easily forget that, relative to what He could have done as God, the all-powerful creator of heaven and earth, Christ did very little. As Evdokimov reminds us: "God limits his almighty power, encloses himself in the silence of his suffering love, withdraws all signs, suspends every miracle, casts a shadow over the brightness of his face."

Sometimes we forget, or maybe we've never really heard or understood, that God redeems us not by being God Almighty in heaven but by becoming a man in Galilee.

In Christ, God enters into human experience and transforms it from within. If we take seriously the Incarnation, we understand that we are redeemed by an act of divine empathy, "for we do not have a high priest who is unable to sympathize with our weaknesses, but we have one who has been tempted in every way, just as we are—yet was without sin" (Hebrews 4:15).

In Jesus Christ, God sees as we see, He lives as we live, and, to quote Evdokimov again, "It is to the humility and empathy of God, of God emptying himself [on the cross] that faith essentially responds. God can do anything — except compel us to love him. Often Christians, in our zeal to proclaim the Gospel, forget that God doesn't force us, but woos us." It is our humble and sincere love that draws people, through us, to Christ Jesus our Lord. Christians must proclaim the gospel; evangelism is essential to our commitment to Jesus Christ. But if we wish to be faithful to Christ's command to us, if we wish to proclaim the gospel with power and authority, it might be better if we do so softly, gently, and with regard for human freedom and dignity.

FR. GREGORY JENSEN is an Eastern Orthodox. A psychologist of religion by profession, he has served rural parishes in northern California, southeast Washington, and western Pennsylvania.

UGLY PREACHING

CASEY TYGRETT / MARCH 10, 2006

I realize even to use this term I'm dragging up a dead set of presuppositions, but in thinking about preaching, teaching, talking, etc., there is for me a state of increasing frustration. Why don't people hear the truth in what I'm saying? Where is the response regarding their lives? We trust in the spirit of truth to really get to the heart of things, but in the end the frustration of someone who undertakes to teach people about the gospel is often intense and mysterious. Each talk, each exposition crafted with hope and care is received as if it were a commencement address: "Good sermon. Not too long." People see it as my job — I see it as a matter of disseminating life-or-death challenges. There is only so long one can dive into and out of this pool before a mental and spiritual funk begins to develop.

In the middle of one such funk, I stumbled onto the passage of Jesus and the parable of the Sower. He gives a grand illustration from the world of agriculture and then lets the whole story close itself. No "in conclusion" or "as we close" needed here — Jesus just told the story and let it hang. The audience and the disciples no doubt twitched nervously, waiting for the exegesis of the story and the resulting invitation to some new commitment or life change. No resolution ever came. Having studied parables, I know they were intended to connect on a real-life level with the hearers. Where's the connection? Did Jesus ever feel as frustrated as today's preachers and teachers?

Later the disciples pulled the explanation out of Jesus but not without this often strange sounding phrase from Isaiah:

they may be ever seeing but never perceiving,
    and ever hearing but never understanding;
    otherwise they might turn and be forgiven! (Mark 4:12)

I suppose that at any point of doubt or crisis, the answer to our conundrum is often quite simple. Jesus' preaching and teaching was simply ugly. It had no neat twists, though it was interesting and the story approach drew people in, and there was little explanation. The reason, prophetically supported, was basically that they need to figure this out for themselves. The secret of the kingdom of God isn't easy to explain and is even more difficult to accept. This message has to be discovered.

I began to examine my own preaching and teaching. I looked at the ways that I communicated and realized that, for the majority of people involved in preaching, the modus operandi has been to completely tie up all the loose ends and send people home feeling as if they have witnessed a verbal dissection and now have portable nuggets of application to either dismiss or embrace as important to their daily existence. I imagine each talk to be a book, which when read from beginning to end leaves no questions or doubts. Everything develops normally and perfectly, and at the end everyone feels better now knowing the perfect answer. How we can rationalize that this is possible, given the fact that we are broken folks giving an unbroken message, is really beyond me. I suppose that is what makes preaching ugly.

And in turn, frustration and stagnation mounts.

What if we make a commitment to preach ugly? If we no longer allow ourselves to be satisfied with complete, easy-to-digest information and instead put the reality on display for people to do with what they wish? Jesus' main objective was to reveal a new covenant and a new relationship with God, but His process did not include giving all the steps and all the understandings necessary to live within that relationship. They were responsible for perceiving, understanding, and turning all by themselves.

The prior commitment to simplified preaching has led to preachers and Christians who are no longer comfortable making decisions without prompting from a lecture filled with exegesis and poetry. What would happen if this ugly preaching became beautiful freedom for Christians everywhere in bondage to easy answers? I believe the preachers and teachers of this world would feel as if chains of spiritual bondage had been lifted. For whatever reason, that spiritual codependency, which involves our emotional health's being based somewhat on the response of people to our presentation of the gospel, would drift helplessly down the drain, while the freedom to simply explicate the problem of mankind interacting with God, without giving obvious and easy-to-accomplish solutions, would become the renewing and powerful event it was intended to be.

My hope is that if I am able to commit to preaching ugly and can avoid the wide path of easy answers, that I will actually provide more answers and direction than ever before. In a time when the tides of culture are shifting, it is only natural that teachers and preachers of the gospel try to focus in on stability and security. Yet what stability does the gospel offer us except a life of trusting, seeking, and growing that is mainly predicated on whether or not we allow ourselves to be affected by and respond to a disgustingly mysterious and beautifully ugly truth? The counter to the frustration of pretty preaching is to let it be ugly — let the shirttails hang out and deliver the gospel unshaven and unkempt into the hearts of individuals who will be helplessly compelled to either hear or understand, see or perceive.

CASEY TYGRETT, his wife Holley, and his new daughter, Bailey, live in central Illinois, where he is involved in preaching and teaching adjunct courses at a local Bible college. The Tygretts are huge music and literature addicts.

RESPONDING

BEFORE I BECAME A TEACHING pastor at Mariner's Church in Irvine, CA, I was the announcement guy. Well, okay, that wasn't my official job title, but for a lot of the congregation, that was my role. I was the host of each service. We had four of them on Sunday morning, plus a Saturday night service, so, to be fair, it wasn't exactly a cushy job.

The Saturday night service was kind of the run-through for the rest of the weekend. The senior pastor, Kenton, the worship leader, and I would all sit down after the service and try to figure out how to make it better before Sunday morning.

Usually the conversation would begin something like this, "So, Spence, what do you think? What should I cut?"

And I'd tell him, usually in no uncertain terms, what I'd change — "that illustration didn't work," "I think you wandered here," "better rethink that point" — you know, pretty much whatever came into my head. Often as I was talking, I'd watch the color wash out of Kenton's face and his shoulders sink a little. But what's a guy to do? If he didn't want my opinion, maybe he shouldn't have asked for it.

Over time, I started to dread those sessions. They just felt awkward, and I began to feel less and less like I was on the same team with him. The tension seemed to carry over in the rest of our relationship as well. Eventually, I just decided to shut up, and for about three months,

I didn't say much of anything.

Finally, Kenton asked me again. "Hey, Spence, what do you think? What should we do?" But this time, instead of telling him what I thought he did wrong, I decided to tell him what I thought he was doing right.

At one point during the message, he came alive, the congregation came alive, and Scripture came alive. It was one of those magical moments that pastors dream about. So I told him what I'd seen. "That part was really great," I said. "You could almost just focus just on that."

The next morning, he got up to speak and gave me a little nod on his way up to the platform. Sure enough, he'd reworked the message to focus on just that one thing. It was incredible, and once again the magic was there (or the anointing, I guess, depending on your perspective).

Things changed after that. Whenever Kenton would ask what he should do differently, I'd tell him about something I thought he was doing right.

I think the same approach can be helpful for all of us in the emerging church conversation. We need to find points of common ground and encourage people with the things we can agree on. For a long time, we weren't doing a very good job of that, to be frank, and often those who would call themselves emerging were known more for what they were against than what they were for.

But in the last few years, I've sensed that is beginning to change. There seems to be less anger among us and more willingness to engage in genuine dialogue.

The fact is we do disagree on a lot of things. And we probably always will, but we need to find ways to love in the midst of those discussions. We need to connect with people, not get into combat sessions with them.

These last articles are an attempt to make sense of the journey and communicate it to other people. What is the emerging church? Who is emerging? What does the term really mean? These next few pages are an attempt to answer those questions and respond to the critics in a positive, affirming way. Please keep in context the year in which these articles were written. Some tend to be more biting earlier in the conversation. Interestingly enough, some of these ideas which were revolutionary at the time they were posted now seem commonly accepted.

Some articles could, no doubt, be even more graceful, but it's a start. As always, we need to go beyond the author's words and listen for his or her heart. It's not an easy task, but it's a necessary one.

TEN REASONS WHY YOUR CHURCH SUCKS

JOHN O'KEEFE / NOVEMBER 3, 2002

About a month ago, I was sitting at my favorite Starbucks with a friend who just recently came back to the church after a long absence. Jack is not the most disciplined believer, but his heart is set for Christ, and his ideas on church are well grounded. He left the church because of "church abuse." You know, when pastors and members think they are better than you and strive to beat you—spiritually and emotionally—into thinking like them. Anyway, we were talking about the then-upcoming possibility of the Tyson fight that would come to Las Vegas if the commission approved his application (which it did not). As we were "talking" (Jack gets heated when he talks Tyson and fighting), an older gentleman came over and joined us at our table. Ignoring me totally, he started a conversation with my friend about nothing, really. Soon the conversation turned to his reason for coming over (and not smoothly I might add): church.

Apparently this man was a local church leader (I never figured out if he was the pastor or not, and Jack wasn't talking). He was wondering why he had not seen Jack in church for a while. My friend smiled and politely told the man that he fell away from the church for a time, but was now attending another church in town. He thanked the man for asking then tried to move back to our conversation. The gentleman asked why he had not returned to "his" church. Jack, again trying to be very polite, tried to tap dance around the question and not give this man both barrels of his emotional sawed-off shotgun. I could tell it was disturbing him, and I could see he was getting a bit uncomfortable. I tried to move the conversation along, but the man looked at me and said, "Would you please stay out of this? This is between Jack and me." I guess he pushed too far with that one, and my friend snapped: "All right. Do you really want me to tell you why?" "Yes," the gentlemen said demandingly. Jack looked at him and tried to explain, but every time he got one word out, the man countered with some obscure reason that had nothing to do with what Jack was saying. He was trying to invalidate my friend's point of view and doing a poor job of it along the way. Finally, as Jack's frustration seemed to get hotter than the steam used to make the foam on our café mochas, he looked the man straight in the face, and as loud as he could said, "Here are the top ten reasons why I think your church sucks." As he started his list, he looked at me, and it was clear he could see my shock—I had never heard him speak that way before. He reached over and touched my arm as if to assure me he was all right and he had been thinking of this for a while and it was now time to get it off his chest.

"First," he said, "your church is totally irrelevant to the community. You all talk a good game, but you do not see the dynamic of the community changing around you.

"Second, your church is filled with poor leaders and overbearing bullies who believe the best way to get anything done is to frighten people. All you have are people who tell us what to do and don't lead us in doing it.

"Third, your church has no vision. You guys are just dead in the water.

"Fourth, your church is old. Your church is filled with old people who have no reason to move ahead. They have more life behind them than they do ahead of them.

"Fifth, your church is inbred. The people my age in your church are all related to the older people so change is impossible. People who are part of the outside don't feel welcomed into the inside to voice an opinion. Your church is filled with mama's boys.

"Sixth, your church is more concerned about image than reality. You all seem to be more concerned with the condition with building than with building the condition of your people. The carpet looks great because no food is allowed near it. The stained glass is wonderful because you spend more money on cleaning and maintaining it than you do on mission work.

"Seventh, your church sees no need for change. You are all happy in your fortress and are not interested in opening your doors to the outside. Evangelism is a dead concept, and 'community' is only those inside the building.

"Eighth, your church doesn't share a relevant message for a relevant time. You're so concerned with doctrine, you are not allowing me to explore the faith and question the unquestionable.

"Ninth, your church doesn't care about me as a person, only as a check-book. Over the time I was with the church I heard more sermons on how much I should be giving and not one on how much you were willing to give up. The only time I had anyone from your church visit me was when 'pledge time' came around and you needed me to increase my giving. It got to the point where I felt no matter what I gave it would never be enough.

"Tenth, your church is all politics and infighting. Things only get done if you can muster enough political support from others to get your point heard, press your issues, and lobby for approval. You have to wheel and deal to get anything done."

Wow. Needless to say I was impressed and a bit confused. The man looked at my friend and said, "Well, we understand Satan has gotten ahold of you and these are not your words, but his. We will be praying for you and keeping in touch to help you return to God's church." My friend just looked at him — he had just spent half an hour giving a point-by-point explanation as to why he left that church, and the man did not hear a word. In fact, he did what most people in his position do; he put it back on my friend as if to say, "We're not wrong; you are. And one day you will see that." The attitude is, "if you question us, it is because you don't understand God and you are not mature in Christ and you need others to pray for you."

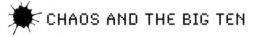

CHAOS AND THE BIG TEN

In chaos theory there is this very cool thing called "turbulence." Now, turbulence is pure destruction. It can best be defined as "destruction inside destruction." If you were to take a snapshot of turbulence and magnify it over and over again, what you would find would be an infinite number of little turbulences inside. Turbulence is turbulence inside turbulence inside turbulence — to an infinite depth. As James Gleick writes in *Chaos: Making a New Science*, "It is a mess of disorder at all scales, small eddies within large ones. It is unstable. It is highly dissipative, meaning that turbulences drains energy and creates drag." With turbulence, it is as if all known rules simply break down and have no meaning. Turbulence will destroy and will damage and will disturb. The question is, just how much?

When air, water, or any object reaches a certain velocity, turbulence will occur — guaranteed. Interestingly, the velocity has nothing to do with increased speed; turbulence can occur on a decrease of speed. It has to do with critical velocity. Ever notice a lit cigarette in an ashtray? See the smooth line of smoke climbing from the cigarette? Watch it for a few seconds and notice that all of a sudden the smooth line of smoke starts to go a little wacky at the top. That is turbulence, a host of eddies forming and causing a mess.

If we look at the church — and not just the one mentioned earlier but all churches — we could get a picture of the turbulence that can cause a church to feed upon itself and die. Here are the top ten reasons given by my friend in his "conversation" with the older gentleman:

1. It does not understand the community at large.
2. It has poor leadership.
3. It has no solid vision.
4. It's graying quickly.
5. It's inbred.
6. It's concerned with appearance and not action.

7. It's comfortable in its misery and is looking for company.
8. It's out of touch with the twenty-first century.
9. It's all about money.
10. It's all politics.

These are the turbulences of the church, the eddies that form the destruction of the church on earth. Like so much of turbulence in chaos theory, these eddies are small and seldom noticed. It is also interesting to note that turbulence is always present. When things are running smoothly, the eddies that form are small and quickly break down. But if the causes of the eddies are ignored, they multiply and become dangerous.

JOHN O'KEEFE holds an MDiv from Drew and is the founder and designer of www.ginkworld.net, an emerging and evolving e-zine designed to help people go deeper in their faith journey. John and his lovely family live in Sacramento, CA, where he is pursuing a doctor of ministry degree and looking for a church to pastor.

JUST WHO IS EMERGENT, ANYWAY?

BOB HYATT / DECEMBER 1, 2005

Because the emerging church conversation/movement is a non-, pan-, cross-, and interdenominational movement, the question arises — "how does one recognize an 'emergent' church?"

This is an important question, particularly as the tide of criticism of all things emergent begins to rise. I find myself, when reading the critics' comments, increasingly thinking, *But what they are describing isn't us!*

If we light a candle, are we emergent? If we meet in a megachurch but are an alternative service, are we emergent? Couches? Book of Common Prayer? Goatees?

This article is not meant to draw lines and declare who is in and who is out. More, it's meant to contribute to the conversation as we all struggle with just what is this thing, anyway?

It may be helpful to think of a continuum of emergence. As I look around, I see three main areas of reconsideration within the emerging church movement. They are methodological, philosophical, and theological, and I want to propose that to the extent that a church community participates in the ongoing reconsideration/dialogue/reformation in each of those areas, they may be considered to a greater or lesser extent emergent.

Many churches which claim to be emergent might better be viewed as a logical continuation of the Willow Creek/Saddleback seeker-sensitive model. They exchange theater seats and a nonthreatening atmosphere for candles and dim lighting, but are mainly concerned about methodological change. They seek methodologies for making themselves more attractive to the unchurched, but ministry philosophy and theology remain largely static. And again, there's nothing wrong with this. God bless them in their mission as they attempt to reach people, right? But emergent? I'm not so sure.

A little farther down the continuum of emergence are the churches rethinking not just methodology but also ministry philosophy. Many of the Acts 29 churches fit in this category. They are willing to change the way that they do things both on an external level (the look and feel of things) and on a deeper level (ministry philosophy, how spiritual formation/discipleship is done), but they aren't really thinking theological change. If anything, many, like Mars Hill in Seattle, actively resist change in the area of theology. They continue to feel comfortable with theological labels such as *Reformed* and continue to subscribe to a view of male-only leadership.

The last (and, I think, most emergent) group of churches out there are the ones who are rethinking all three categories. For them, being emergent isn't just about how Sunday morning is done (methodology), and neither is it simply a matter of changing how things like discipleship and teaching are done (ministry philosophy). It's also a matter of continuing the work of theological discovery. They are rethinking and reforming theology. For them, theology is not a finished work. They take to heart Doug Pagitt's words, "If you want to honor the Reformers, don't just say what they said. . . . Do what they did." This last group not only see the work of contextualizing the knowledge we have of God as a continuing process but also recognize that we don't know all there is to know about God, Scripture, or theology. We think the process of learning more will continue indefinitely—the church will continue to grow in its knowledge of God.

So that's my definition. What do *you* think?

BOB HYATT is the husband of Amy and the father of Jack and Jane. He's also the lead pastor of the Evergreen Community in Portland, OR.

WHAT IS IT ALL ABOUT?

SPENCER BURKE / DECEMBER 20, 2002

In. Out. Together. No, they're not random words from the dictionary or even lyrics from "The Hokey Pokey." They're actually key ideas from the current church conversation. Answers, perhaps, to the often nebulous "what's it all about" question.

I don't know about you, but I've spent a great deal of time this year trying to figure out yet again just what a church is supposed to be — and, more specifically, what characterizes the emerging church.

Let's face it. There are a million rabbit trails one could walk in the emerging/postmodern conversation — everything from worship styles to theological beliefs. Yet, to be honest, I'm not sure agreement — or lack of agreement — in these areas is what necessarily makes a church emerging. While deconstruction is valuable, it's important that we press on to the next stage of the process — the point where we can say, "Here's what we are," not just, "Here's what we're not."

So back to the three words. It seems to me that the essence of the emerging church movement and even the essence of the church itself can be expressed in three ideas: an inward journey, an outward journey, and a journey together. Everything else about our churches — their sizes, shapes, structures, and so forth — is secondary and maybe even irrelevant.

 AN INWARD JOURNEY

A few years back, I had the privilege of going on a silent retreat with Brennan Manning. During that time, I had no choice but to face my fears. Unable to distract myself with the business of pastoring, I came to see just how much I had been hiding from God and how often I had recoiled from taking the inward journey. Alone in the quiet that week, I began to wrestle with God. Possibly for the first time in my life, I was truly honest with my Creator. I let the real cries of my heart be known and through that time came to experience the love of Christ in a way I never had before.

In the emerging church, we're seeing a renewed interest in things like contemplation, prayer, meditation, and spiritual direction. I'm encouraged by this trend because I think these inward practices can go a long way in helping us become the people God has called us to be. The more we can do to encourage people to take the inward journey—to wrestle with God and face their fears on a daily basis—the better off I think we'll be. We need to help people get "unstuck," whether through contemplation, intensive healing prayer, or something else. And the reality is that growing through the inward journey is a lifelong struggle. A retreat or two is good, but true discipleship means working out our faith over the long-haul. It is, after all, a journey.

 AN OUTWARD JOURNEY

As in a labyrinth, the inward journey is followed by an outward journey. For me, facing my fears and experiencing intimacy with God has given me a greater freedom to live out my calling: being in a real world, with real people, in real time. I no longer have the desire to be at the top of some church hierarchy or corporate ladder, but instead, I desire to become a servant. Through some mystical process, my heart is changing. From time to time, I'm actually able to embrace not only my own brokenness but the brokenness of others as well. I can now come alongside people and travel with them. Rather than wanting to fix them, I can simply be with them and allow God to work through me.

 A JOURNEY TOGETHER

Community is a big deal in the emerging church. We're desperate for authentic relationships and a sense of belonging that extends beyond a Sunday handshake at the door.

The present incarnation of Christ is the church. We are not alone in our struggles, nor are we the only ones walking the labyrinth. Whether we are part of a house church or a megachurch, we are ultimately part of *the* church. Budgets, formulas, programs — they're incidental. If the focus of the emerging church is just three things: the inward journey, the outward journey, and the journey together, we have a common, unifying bond.

Just the same, many of us need details. We can accept the "in, out, together" idea at a high level, but we need to know what it really looks like in everyday life. I'm not exactly sure, but here are some ways the inward and outward journeys might come together in your world.

ACTS OF CONTEMPLATION AND COMPASSION

Acts of contemplation can be anything from silent retreat and meditation, to lectio divina and small group participation. Counseling and spiritual direction also fit here. The focus is on studying God's Word more for life change than academic enrichment.

Acts of compassion, meanwhile, are a natural balance to contemplation. They encourage us not just to reflect on truth but also to live it. As we allow God to change our hearts, we begin to live differently. Acts of compassion may be as simple as going down to a local park with a meal and inviting those who are hungry to join us, or as complex as responding to a world infected with AIDS. Each act is about going into the wider community and meeting a real need.

THEOLOGY AND THE ARTS

We need to rediscover what it means to think *and* to feel. A fresh look at theology may mean asking deeper questions and re-examining the words of Christ. What was Jesus really trying to say through the kingdom parables? Is there more to the story of Jesus than just atonement? Perhaps a missional calling that has been overlooked?

The arts, meanwhile, encourage us to learn through other means — to know by using our senses. The arts — whether high- or lowbrow — speak to us at a soul level. We embrace the opportunity to learn about life from films, novels, all kinds of creative expressions. We're open to both experiencing these art forms and creating pieces of our own.

COMMUNITY AND PERSONAL STEWARDSHIP

As the emerging church, we can also look for ways to build healthy communities. We may concern ourselves with issues of social justice, mental, and physical health or even the environment. Perhaps it's time we took a hard look at the definitions of poverty and gluttony, for instance, and challenged the principles that guide our daily lives. Could our world really sustain itself if every nation embraced North American rates of consumption? Stewardship means learning how to care for the people around us — in our neighborhoods and around the world.

Our interest in community is balanced by personal stewardship. We take a holistic approach to health and sexuality. We don't divorce the body from the soul or compartmentalize aspects of our lives. Instead, we look at the whole person and consider the complexities of what it means to be human. We not only care for others, we also care for ourselves.

So what do you think? Is the "in, out, and together" concept a good definition for the emerging church — or even the church as a whole? Is it something that we can rally around no matter what our particular religious stripe?

I invite you to share your thoughts. Drop me an email at Spencer@ TheOoze.com or stop in at TheOOZE message boards: www.theooze. com/forums/index.cfm. Let's keep the conversation going.

In the 1990s, Spencer created TheOOZE.com to be a safe online community for a diverse faith-based population to connect through articles, message boards, and social networking. Spencer lives with Lisa, his wife of twenty years, and children, Alden (nine) and Grace (five) in Southern California.

THE SKINNY ON POSTMODERNITY SERIES, PART I

Postmodernism and Global Worldviews

ANDREW JONES / MARCH 27, 2002

Critics who target their attacks on postmodernism find their subject moving too fast to set their sights. Settlers who want the postmodern paradigm to last forever will be disappointed.

Postmodernity is not a permanent fixture. It is not a place to land. There is no real estate to build on, no viewpoint stationary enough to camp out on. It is a world in transition, a tunnel to the next global metaphysic, a vehicle that will transport its party to another way of thinking — one that will resonate with the new realities. Any theology we create in this time of chaotic evolution must be located to the minute and the day as well as to the piece of ground we walk on.

I keep saying these things, yet many people are convinced that postmodernity is the enemy territory, the new Jericho to march around and blow trumpets at in the hope that its walls will collapse inward and crush its Rahab-esque inhabitants with righteous judgment. In this skinny on global worldviews, I really just want to locate the postmodern mindset in relation to the other worldviews, showing its place as a transitional, seasonal worldview, and necessary step to the next dominant metaphysic.

A good place to start is in the oldest book of the Bible, the book of Job.

JOB AND THREE UNHELPFUL FRIENDS

The book of Job enjoys renewed popularity thanks to its postmodern allowance for mystery, suffering, paradox, and unanswered questions. Many young people find that Job's account resonates with their own experience of life. I find even more —that in the account of the righteous man Job and his odyssey to discover the cause of his suffering and loss, this old man with the peeling scabs encounters the basic global world-views that have dominated history since the beginning.

Toward the beginning of Job's suffering, just when his scabs were calling for attention, three friends sit with him and help him think through what the cause might be. These friends are Bildad, Zophar and Eliphaz. In their explanations for why God is allowing disease and death, I find the basic metaphysical efforts of people around the world, despite geography, history, and religion.

Basically, I see three major worldviews, three ways of thinking that may have always dominated eras of history. Here they are:

1. Traditional. Bildad responds to Job by asking what the fathers have said about the situation because there was nothing new to be learned. He is a traditionalist, and he looks back in history to find what others have already said. He has a high regard for truth and sees it as inherited, not to be messed with, something wrestled over by the elders, handed down to those eager for wisdom, and eventually passed on to the next generation.

2. Rational. Zophar appeals to rational wisdom and hints that Job is "witless" or stupid. He also gives a formula that if Job does certain things, then a favorable outcome will result. His approach would be considered modern in today's understanding of the world. Modern thinkers see truth as something available to those who are willing to work hard to find it. Truth gives itself to diligent study, methodical inquiry,

unbiased interrogation. Truth evades the foolish and cannot be passed on through good breeding. It responds to scientific methods of discovery and can be proved on scientific grounds. Here we have the basic Enlightenment paradigm and the dominant western worldview for the past two hundred years.

3. Mystical. Eliphaz appeals to his experiences to prove his point. He had a dream, and his hair stood on end. A spirit appeared. This was proof enough. He sees God as one who "performs wonders that cannot be fathomed" (Job 5:9). He sees truth as something elusive, beyond the reach of mortal men who are bound in the material world, limited by the senses and the boundaries of existence. Truth to Eliphaz and to millions around the world is available only in short glimpses and at special times when the dimensions meet, in the time between times, in the gap moments of revelation and enlightenment.

A funny thing about the book of Job is that each guy, with such radically differing thought processes, comes to the same conclusion: Job has sinned and is therefore suffering. Even funnier is the fact that all three men are wrong. The truth in this case is something more complicated and mysterious. But watching them think is worth the exercise because they represent how people think in general.

 BACK TO ELIPHAZ

I believe that Eliphaz represents the worldview that is becoming predominant around the world and will one day become the leading global metaphysic. Eliphaz is somewhat of a mystic and represents a mindset that is more common in eastern thinking than in western, although our world is becoming post-western by the minute. He is occupied with the power encounters of God (see 4:9), God's activity in the natural world (see 4:10), and the need for justice for the poor (see 5:15-16). Understanding

Eliphaz is a key to understanding how people in the Western world are beginning to think. The new mindset represents a change in the way we approach knowledge, truth, and how we explain things to people with a differing value system.

Is Eliphaz postmodern? I say no. He represents something of where we are going rather than where we are now. I will explain shortly, but I need to flesh out the three worldviews first.

 THREE AND NO MORE

These three worldviews were first brought to my attention by Dr. J. Carl Laney of Western Conservative Baptist Seminary, during my time as a student there in the 1980s. Laney suggested that Bildad was a traditionalist, Zophar a rationalist. Eliphaz, he called a mystic. He did not present them as global mindsets. Perhaps I took his teaching more seriously than he did. But I have been road testing them now for twelve years and still see them as the three primary metaphysics active in today's world. I have also found them in various forms in the teachings of other people I have encountered since Dr. Laney.

For example: Jim Petersen spent a weekend with us at a retreat in Oregon. He suggested that a major worldview shift was taking place. We have already moved, he claimed, from a God-centered worldview (pre-modern) to a man-centered worldview. We are now moving to an environment-centered worldview. This would fit with traditional, rational, and mystical.

Brother Thomas Wolf, missiologist and teacher, sees Paul ministering to three mindsets in the book of Acts: The Hebrews [traditionalists] in Acts 13, whom he addresses in Aramaic and starts with the story of "our fathers" (verse 17). The Athenians [rationalists] in Acts 17 who receive from Paul a rational defense of the gospel and appropriate steps to take (repentance). And the mystical Lystrans in Acts 14, to whom Paul has to explain the healing/power-encounter so that they do not worship him. He tells them it is the same God who has already been speaking to them in the past by sending them rain. These would be the mystics.

Paul Ray, from the Institute of Noetic Sciences, came up with three groupings of American people in the midnineties. The Traditionals (29 percent) who are usually older; The Moderns (47 percent), who make up the mainstream; and Cultural Creatives (24 percent), who represent the emerging culture and are the only group that is growing. His studies show that the Traditionals have much in common with the Cultural Creatives.

Ray divides the Cultural Creatives into two groups: the Greens (13 percent of the U.S. adult population), who focus on social and environmental issues; and the Core Cultural Creatives (11 percent), who value spiritual integration. This Core group is composed of the leading edge thinkers, says Ray, and twice as many of them are women than men.[1]

Willis Harman, in his book *Global Mind Change* simplifies metaphysics to three basic ways of seeing reality:

- M1: Materialistic Monism (matter gives rise to mind). The stuff of the universe teaches us about reality.
- M2: Dualism (matter plus mind). Matter-energy stuff and mind-spirit stuff are two complementary knowledge sources.
- M3: Transcendental Monism (mind gives rise to matter). It is this mindset that sees deep intuition and consciousness as preceding any material evolution and products.

Harman's observation is that we are moving from an M1 mindset to M3. In the M3 mindset, preference is given to the unconscious and dreams.[2] As it is stated in the book *A Course in Miracles*, "Everything you see is the result of your thoughts."[3]

Again, this fits with the traditional, rational and mystical.

✴ BUT WHAT ABOUT THE POSTMODERN?

Okay, this is what I believe: Cultures do not shift immediately from one major paradigm to the next. There is a transitional period that includes a rethinking of the previous paradigm, an acknowledgement of its limitations, a deconstruction, an exploration of new thinking to explain a new reality, an adoption of new ideas, a remixing of multiple viewpoints, and eventually a radically different group consensus. This transition period could last a hundred years before the majority of people hold a new dominant paradigm.

I believe we are in such a time as this — possibly halfway through, if this change started in the 1960s. Paul Ray believes that in the early 1960s, only 4 percent held to the value system of the Cultural Creatives. Today a quarter of Americans would hold to that paradigm and no doubt the number would be much higher among youth, artists, and media influencers. Brian MacLaren says that 80 percent of young people have already transitioned into a postmodern mindset and 20 percent of older people. Postmodernity is the water we swim in. It is not a case of whether we like it or not. Or agree with it or not. It is here. It exists. It just *is*.

However — and this will come as good news to some — I believe that postmodernity is a transitional period, and what we are moving into will be different again. Not completely different, since there are elements in postmodern thinking that will be here to stay. But our journey is a long one, and we have not reached shore yet. The transition from one way of thinking to another does not come smoothly. There is always an intermediate step, a series of experimental convictions that allows the new. We will be in the postmodern world for some time, and it is essential that we come to grips with it and learn how to function in it. Just as our ancestors came up with *Good News for Modern Man*, we also must find the good news for postmodern people. Functioning and even succeeding in the postmodern world is not as hard as it seems. In fact, a world in transition is generally more open to change and new things than a world stuck in the status quo of a dominant worldview. Explaining the mystery of the gospel should be easier for us now than it has been for a really long time.

POSTMODERNISM IN THE CONTEXT OF GLOBAL WORLDVIEWS

If there are three dominant mindsets, then there is at least one other worldview that would represent the transition from one to another. If this transition takes time, which I believe it does, then the transitional mindset becomes in many cases a worldview of its own, although more dynamic than static. In our world, we are calling it postmodernism, since we are leaving the modern worldview and will one day adopt another. In the account of Job, the flow of conversation is interrupted by a young man who, after waiting his turn to speak, tells Job that the other three men are wrong. The young obnoxious man is Elihu. I see Elihu as representing the transitional, which in today's world is the postmodern. There is a pregnant moment when Elihu comes closer to the truth than the three older men. And yet he also is proved to be wrong. In my mind, Elihu personifies the deconstructive, the doubt-casting, idol-dethroning, paradigm-shattering attack on the status quo. It is Elihu who is the postmodern hero of the book of Job.

ELIHU: POSTMODERN HERO

The thinking of Elihu is the vehicle that allows contemplation, suspicion, deconstruction, and the way to think in another dimension. This is his advice to the suffering Job:

> For the ear tests words
>> as the tongue tastes food.
> Let us discern for ourselves what is right;
>> let us learn together what is good. (Job 34:3-4)

Here we have three elements of postmodern thinking. The suspicious testing of what seems right. The commitment to the local community to discern for ourselves. And the value of collaboration in learning together. I see in Elihu the postmodern tension of today, the conflict of living and thinking in between worldviews. For it is my opinion that we are moving from a Zophar (rational) way of thinking to a more Eliphaz (mystical/experiential) way of thinking. One that is more eastern than western, more Hebraic than Greek. One in which experience precedes explanation rather than follows it. Rather than attacking the shortcomings of postmodern thinking, we might do better to prepare people for the worldview around the corner, one which is showing us glimpses of itself.

POSTMODERNISM: WORLDVIEW NUMBER FOUR?

Walter Truett Anderson includes the postmodern in his set of four ways of thinking. Anderson's first three fit in with the previous sets I have mentioned.

1. Social-traditional, in which truth is found in the heritage of previous learning.
2. Scientific-rational, in which truth is found through methodical inquiry.
3. Neo-Romantic, in which truth is found either by "attaining harmony with nature and/or spiritual exploration of the inner self."[4]

Again, these three line up with Job's three friends. But Anderson adds another worldview:

4. Postmodern-ironist, which sees truth as not found at all but made or socially constructed.[5] Anderson's distinction between finding truth and making truth is valuable. All truth

in its man-made packaging is somehow constructed by someone.

✸ THREE KINDS OF POSTMODERNS

It is also important to note that there is not a singular "postmodern" but many postmoderns and many postmodernists. For the sake of simplicity, there are basically three postmodern positions at this point in time.

Pauline Marie Rosenau, professor of political science at the University of Quebec, has done a great work in naming the distinctions that separate the first two groups of postmodern thinkers, who she calls "skeptics" and "affirmatives."

1. Skeptical Postmodernists offer a pessimistic and gloomy scenario. They are inspired by early Continental postmodernism (Heidegger and Nietzsche) and focus on chaos, death, and the impossibility of truth. It is these early authors who were picked up by Christian teachers as representative of postmodernism in general; a very unhealthy and unfair critique which has made it difficult for dialogue to take place among Christian intellectual communities.

2. Affirmative Postmodernists offer a more optimistic view of the postmodern transition, though they may agree with the skeptics' critique of modernity. They are more influenced by North American and British authors. They affirm an ethical system. They value choices that are superior and are open to honest intellectual practice. This is more reflective of the Christian teachers who are training students to minister in a postmodern world.

Rosenau acknowledges that there are some postmodernists who avoid the label since the word *postmodern* promotes a singular view of reality, encourages closure, and denies complexity. Although she doesn't give a name to this group in the short article of hers I am reading, others often call this group "post-postmodern" or "po-po-mo." I don't like the term since it sounds too reactive of modernity. People in this third category are no longer defined by what they came out of but by where they are now and where they are heading. In line with Rosenau's other labels, an appropriate name that I would ascribe to this third set would be Intuitive Postmoderns.

Anderson also sees three kinds of postmodernists: He names them the Nihilist, the Constructivist, and the Player. The Player, like the Intuitive, finds it natural and effortless to cruise this new world and find success in it.

Douglas Ruskoff, in his excellent book *Playing the Future* would call the last one a "Surfer" rather than a Player. Rushkoff describes Surfers as those who see the deeper order in the chaos around them and learn instinctively how to surf the patterns and move through life. He goes as far to say that surfers (the kind at the beach with surfboards) were the first postmodernists. If Christians were reading Douglas Rushkoff in the 1990s rather than Douglas Coupland, then we might have not camped out so long in the skeptical mode.

Brad Sargent, of Golden Gate Theologial Seminary, also sees three distinct postmodern thinkers and gives examples of them.

1. New Edge, as personified by the punks of the 1970s.
2. Far Edge, like the cyber-punks of the 1990s.
3. Over The Edge, like the global nomads and third-culture kids of the emerging global culture. Many missionaries' kids, Sargent adds, would fall under this category since they have learned to function in multiple environments.[6]

In my own explanation of the various stages of the postmodern transition, I found it helpful to use the following concepts:

1. Barn-Burning: a sometimes angry or resentful deconstruction to delete what should not be there
2. Dumpster-Diving: an inquisitive exploration to discover and restore what was missing, hidden, or forbidden
3. Well, I don't have a good word for this stage, actually. I was using Lego-Land but am not happy with it. Consider the naming of this stage as a work in progress. But even without a label, this final stage of the transitional process represents a creative remixing of the new and old elements to construct a new and better way.

Brian McLaren, a leading Christian teacher on this topic, often explains the transition using these same three stages that I shared with him, even though the last one lacks a title.

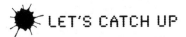 LET'S CATCH UP

There are three major worldviews, and, at the risk of oversimplification and a shameless reductionism, we could sum them up like this. They are:

1. Traditionists, who inherit truth
2. Rationalists, who discover truth
3. Mystics, who experience truth

And, if we include the present transitional postmodern mindset,

4. Postmodernists, who construct truth

Of course the postmodernists would say that everyone constructs truth, based on their own background, disposition, and bias. But the postmodernist is the one who admits it and would not take their own construct as seriously as the others. The posture toward man-made truth is more humble, suspicious, and playful, in the acknowledgment that everything made by human hands is suspect. That goes for our sermons, books, theologies.

Even our statements of faith are tainted by prejudice and therefore under suspicion. This leads us to affirm the words of the famous hymn:

> I dare not trust the sweetest frame [construct],
> But wholly lean on Jesus' name.
> On Christ the Solid Rock I stand,
> All other ground is sinking sand.
> All other ground is sinking sand.

So right about here is where the traditionalists and modernists chime in with their attack on postmodern thinking. Is there a truth that is really true? Absolutely true? (They like that word, *absolute*.) And there is not one single correct postmodern answer, since, as I have said, there are many postmodernists and not all of them would agree with my stance. But let me answer it my way.

Yes, there is truth. But truth is found in Someone, not something. God is truth. His Word is truth. God never changes. He will always be true. God is also beyond time and space and the small boundaries of human definitions. But we are bound by time and space and see through a glass dimly, at least on this side of eternity, which humbles us in our intellectual treatises and makes us more dependent on God to reveal Himself. It also removes us from an unhealthy dependency (idolatry?) upon scientific methods to determine correct interpretations. It drives us toward faith in God—to depend on His Spirit to lead us, to protect the sanctity of the mystery of God, to value the role of creation as a co-revealer of God, to be holistic in striving toward truth, to trust in each other as the community of God (*ecclesia*). All in all, to be faithful to God and each other in this postmodern world means to be people of faith, people who are holy (wholly) just as God is holy, people who refuse to downsize God by reductionist explanations. We are moving from dualism to holism, piecing things together rather than pulling them apart. Humility and honesty in our attempts to discover and communicate truth.

Elihu says it well.

How great is God — beyond our understanding!
The number of his years is past finding out.
. . . .

Who can understand how he spreads out the clouds?
(Job 36:26,29)

SO . . .

It is probably true that we are halfway through a major global paradigm shift. The time of Eliphaz is almost upon us. From a rational world of highly processed truth that gives way easily under human inquiry to a world of mysterious, elusive truth that lies hidden in nature and peeks out occasionally through power encounters, dreams, revelation, and the truth that resonates in what is really Real. We are presently experiencing the chaos of transition out of modernism and into something that is, as yet, undefined. The time of transition is one in which we cannot land anywhere for very long, cannot see everything clearly. We need to have faith in what is unseen, to rest in God's ability to lead us. As Job says "But he knows the way that I take; when he has tested me, I will come forth as gold" (23:10).

ANDREW JONES directs The Boaz Project and is the postmodern consultant for the Baptist General Convention of Texas. He blogs daily at tallskinnykiwi.typepad.com. This article is part one in the Skinny Series, which is a work in progress, and your input is appreciated. You can read the other articles in the series at TheOOZE.com and send comments to tallskinnykiwi@hotmail.com.

THE ERA OF ANTICIPATION

ANDREW HUBBARD / MAY 29, 2005

Charles Colson wrote an article in *Christianity Today* that stated that postmodernism is dying. Brian McLaren responded to it, and said that Colson had a mistaken view of postmodernism. Colson wrote an e-mail back, but McLaren decided not to respond any further. I've read books by both authors and highly respect both of them.

When I read the articles, I tended to agree with Colson more than McLaren. But Colson has a skewed view of postmodernism, especially in a Christian context. I believe that God is using postmodernism to bring people back to the feet of Jesus, where there is fullness of joy. He's bringing His people back to His presence, back to faith, and back to an unconformable gospel. I don't think that postmoderns, as Colson thinks, have given up on the truth. They are in search of the truth, and they are confused by the numerous options. They're stuck at the Subway counter because they don't know what condiments they want on their sub. And so they are pursuing the truth; they are looking and seeking, but they have come to realize that it is not easy. And so it is true that postmoderns (even postmodern Christians) are slow to attach themselves to doctrine or beliefs.

Christian postmoderns have found that they themselves have changed with the times, that they don't think like their parents. Perhaps they think this way because they have grown up on TV and junk food and all that other stuff. But they've found something that energizes them. They find that they can truly learn from movies and stories and paintings and colors. Not only that, but they have realized that they can express themselves to God through these media.

Postmodern Christians have discovered that they can't discover everything about God. They can't fathom how deep, wide, and massive God's love for them is, and they are okay with this. They have not given up in their pursuit of the truth, but they have found a wonder that was lost in the Modern age.

And so they express their love and emotions to God through paintings, poetry, and stories. *Narrative*, I believe, is a term that is being tossed around. Strangely, I find that this is the way that Jesus Himself represented the kingdom and the kingdom values. He used parables and stories and hyperbole and all that stuff to show how God's kingdom works.

I believe that God is arousing the anticipation of people in this age of postmodernism. And I believe that God wants to build up leaders who would follow Him wholeheartedly. I believe that God is calling for leaders who lead by example, leaders who move people because they believe and demonstrate the truth of God and that "he gave his one and only Son, that whoever believes in him shall not perish but have eternal life" (John 3:16). God is raising up people young and old who will embody the good news. They will bear the marks of their savior's love and so, like Paul, fill up "what is still lacking in regard to Christ's afflictions" (Colossians 1:24).

Only God and His prophets know what the Postmodern Era is (and only history will prove if there is, in fact, a Postmodern Era), how long it will last, and if it is a short time of transition. Whatever the case, God uses shifts in thinking for His glory. And so, of course, it is a transition point just as every other age has been. God continues to thwart the plans of men and to continue on with His plan of salvation and redemption. Praise God for His sovereign plans.

I pray that Christians would not swing so freely as the pendulum that the world swings on. Let us stay centered in Christ rather than swaying to and fro with different ideologies and motivations. Let us use the culture at hand to portray the message but not be afraid to jump out of the box and challenge culture. Struggle with the ideas of grace and discipline until they line up in a Christ-centered way.

We are to be "little Christs." We are to be bringers of peace and bringers of the sword. We are to lead as Christ led and to suffer as Christ suffered. We are to serve and to stand up. We are to turn the other cheek and also to fight "the prince of the power of the air" (Ephesians 2:2, KJV). We are to be as innocent as doves and as shrewd as snakes. All this so that God might be glorified by the joy that we've found in Him and that God might be glorified by our joy in Him that has been increased by the joy that others have found in Him.

The Modern Era was a time for the mind, but the Postmodern Era seems to be a time for the heart. I pray that, as God touches our hearts, we would also love Him by giving Him all of our souls, our minds, and our strength too. God, as far as I can tell, is holistic. He wants the whole thing, but it seems that we people can only handle a little bit at a time. Let this time turn from confusion and busyness of ideas to simplicity of faith. Let this be a time of resting in grace and pursuing His glory.

ANDREW HUBBARD currently lives in Calgary, Canada, where, with the (necessary) patience and encouragement of his family and girlfriend, he hopes to influence people with the good news of Jesus Christ. Andrew blogs at www.xanga.com/ahub. Andrew is moody, doesn't drink much coffee, and loves great conversations.

CONCLUSION

SOME OF YOU ARE DISAPPOINTED right now. You're disappointed I didn't write more. You're disappointed that the articles didn't give more how-tos and practical tips. You wanted a comprehensive guide to the emerging journey; instead, you got a stack of somewhat random post-cards from a motley group of travelers.

The good news is that this isn't the end of the story. TheOOZE is, after all, an online community. The articles selected for this book are a mere offline sample of what's available online. Every day new articles are posted and new comments added. It's definitely a work in process.

Would you like to respond to one of the articles reprinted here? Would you like to add your perspective on an issue or ask the author to clarify a point? You can, just by logging on at TheOOZE.com.

I fear that sounds like a commercial, but it isn't meant to be. I'm not meaning to promise that logging onto TheOOZE.com will get your whites whiter or your brights brighter. I can't even promise that it will freshen your breath. But it will, I believe, challenge your thinking in ways a static book — even one as provocative as this one — can't.

I've been doing a lot of radio interviews this last year, and often the hosts are unrelenting in their quest for a great sound bite. On one particular show, I was asked about who was really leading the emerging movement. Was it me? Was it Brian McLaren? Was it Leonard Sweet? It was an impossible question to respond to — so I said the first thing that popped into my head: "I feel like Al Gore, claiming to have invented the Internet."

The truth is Al Gore didn't invent the Internet, and I'm not the leader of this thing. I don't think Brian McLaren or Leonard Sweet is the leader either. This truly is a collaborative journey we're on. Every one is contributing and adding his or her unique voice.

A while ago, I was shocked to see that someone had posted an article on TheOOZE questioning whether global warming was a real phenomenon and what Christians' response to it should be. Even worse, the article was submitted on Earth Day. I have to tell you, everything within me wanted to pull the article off the database when I saw it, but I refrained because that's not my role. I facilitate the conversation; I don't censor it.

You might have noticed comments on the article, "A Tiny Female Emergent Voice." We allow community members to comment on the articles that are posted because we believe that feedback and dialogue are good. They help move us forward. They challenge us to a higher level of thinking and engagement.

Earlier I mentioned the graffitied walls that seem to be springing up everywhere these days. It's a picture of what's happening in the emerging church conversation generally and on TheOOZE specifically. The work doesn't belong to any one artist. Each person who comes along adds a little something or takes a little something away in hopes of improving the overall piece. They're unlikely artists working on an unlikely canvas. They're not cordoning off sections of the piece and stamping a big copyright mark on it. They're just journeying together, trying to follow God as best they know how.

At TheOOZE, anyone is welcome to grab a can of spray paint and join in the conversation. Anyone is welcome to take the component pieces and remix them in a new way. Sometimes the results will be ugly. Sometimes the process will be messy. But it's in that process that hope is found.

NOTES

DETOXING FROM CHURCH

1. Dallas Willard, *Renovation of the Heart: Putting on the Character of Christ* (Colorado Springs, CO: NavPress, 2002), 85.
2. Willard, 87.
3. Willard, 248.
4. Willard, 89.
5. Willard, 85.
6. See Willard, 240-251, for a fuller discussion of these aspects.
7. Dallas Willard, *The Divine Conspiracy: Rediscovering Our Hidden Life in God* (San Francisco: HarperSanFrancisco, 1998), 236.

PARADIME

1. David K. Naugle, Worldview: *The History of a Concept* (Grand Rapids, MI: Eerdman's, 2002), 5.
2. Brian D. McLaren, *More Ready Than You Realize: Evangelism As Dance in the Postmodern Matrix* (Grand Rapids, MI: Zondervan, 2002), 148.
3. McLaren, 131.
4. Philip Jenkins, *The Next Christendom: The Coming of Global Christianity* (New York: Oxford University Press, 2002), 220.
5. Charles Colson and Nancy Pearcey, *How Now Shall We Live?* (Wheaton, IL: Tyndale, 1999), 15.
6. Colson and Pearcey, 16.
7. Charles Colson and Ellen Vaughn, *Being the Body: A New Call for the Church*

to Be Light in the Darkness (Nashville: W Publishing, 2003), 210.

8. George Barna, *Think Like Jesus: Make the Right Decision Every Time* (Nashville: Integrity, 2003), 40.

9. George Barna and The Barna Group, "The State of the Church: 2005" (Ventura, CA: The Barna Group, 2005), 51.

10. Leonard Sweet, *Out of the Question . . . into the Mystery: Getting Lost in the GodLife Relationship* (Colorado Springs, CO: WaterBrook, 2004), 20–21.

11. McLaren, 50.

12. Donald Miller, *Searching for God Knows What* (Nashville: Thomas Nelson, 2004), 57.

13. Dallas Willard, *The Divine Conspiracy: Rediscovering Our Hidden Life in God* (San Francisco: HarperSanFrancisco, 1998), 153.

14. Francis Schaeffer, *True Spirituality* (Wheaton, IL: Tyndale, 1971), 128.

15. Tony Campolo, *Who Switched the Price Tags?* (Nashville: W Publishing, 1986), 148–149.

16. Sweet, 31.

17. McLaren, 84.

18. Robert N. Bellah, et al, *Habits of the Heart: Individualism and Commitment in American Life* (Berkley, CA: University of California Press Berkeley, 1985 and 1996), 296.

19. Donald Miller, *Blue Like Jazz: Nonreligious Thoughts on Christian Spirituality* (Nashville: Thomas Nelson, 2003), 110–111.

20. James Emery White, *Rethinking the Church* (Grand Rapids, MI: Baker Books, 2001), 151.

21. Brian McLaren, *Finding Faith: A Self-Discovery Guide for Your Spiritual Quest* (Grand Rapids, MI: Zondervan, 2003), 13–14.

22. Barna, *Think Like Jesus*, 40.

THE PARADOX OF A DIVIDED CHURCH CALLED TO BE RECONCILERS TO THE WORLD

1. Michael Riddell, *Threshold of the Future: Reforming the Church in the Post-Christian West* (London: Society for Promoting Christian Knowledge, 1998), 57.

2. Riddell, 61.

3. Jürgen Moltmann, *The Open Church: Invitation to a Messianic Lifestyle* (London: SCM Press, 1978), 29.

4. Moltmann, 29.

5. Alan Jamieson, *A Churchless Faith: Faith Journeys Beyond the Churches* (Cleveland, OH: Pilgrim, 2002), 40.

6. Riddell, 69.

7. Henri Nouwen, *In the Name of Jesus* (London: Darton, Longman, and Todd, 1989), 63.

8. Nouwen, 45.

9. Larry Crabb, *Connecting: Healing for Ourselves and Our Relationships* (Nashville: W Publishing, 1997), 10.

10. The term here, *katapetasma*, is not entirely clear. It could refer to the curtain separating the holy of holies from the holy place as Josephus says, or it could refer to one at the entrance of the temple courts. Many commentators argue that the inner curtain is meant because another term, *kalumma*, is also used for the outer curtain. Others see a reference to the other curtain as more likely because of the public nature of this sign. I take it to mean holy of holies, but in both cases the issue is the same: Access to God has been opened up.

WAKE UP, CHURCH, AND SMELL THE COFFEE

1. http://www.handguncontrol.org.

JACKSON, GOD, AND ME

1. Steven Naifeh and Gregory White Smith, *Jackson Pollock: An American Saga*, 3rd ed. (New York: Woodward/White, 1998), 539.

2. Vladimir Lossky, *Mystical Theology of the Eastern Church* (Crestwood, NY: St.Vladimir's Seminary Press, 1997), 25.

LEADING FROM THE MARGINS

1. Christopher Alexander, interview on CBC Radio, IDEAS. Fall, 2002. http://www.cbc.ca/ideas.

2. Walter Brueggemann, *Finally Comes the Poet* (Minneapolis, MN: Augsburg, 1989).

3. T. E. Lawrence, *The Seven Pillars of Wisdom* (New York: Doubleday, 1991).

4. Alan Roxburgh, *The Sky is Falling* (Eagle, ID: ACI Publishing, 2006), 167.

5. Elisabeth Fiorenza, quoted by Rosemary Neave in "Reimagining the Church," Study Leave Report for the Women's Resource Center, NZ, 1996.

6. Michael Frost and Alan Hirsch, *The Shaping of Things to Come* (Massachusetts, PA: Hendrickson, 2003), 188.

7. Fritjof Capra quoted in Frost and Hirsch, 122.

8. Alan Roxburgh, blog, May 2006, http://odyssey.blogs.com.

THE SKINNY ON POSTMODERNITY

1. Paul Ray, interview for ONN, 1998.

2. Willis Harman, *Global Mind Change: The Promise of the Twenty-First Century* (Petaluma, CA: Institute of Noetic Sciences, 1998).

3. The Foundation for Inner Peace, *A Course in Miracles* (Wisconsin Dells, WI: New Christian Church of Full Endeavor, 2005), 775.

4. *The Truth About Truth: De-Confusing and Re-Constructing the Postmodern World*, Walter Truett Anderson, ed. (New York: Putnam, 1995), 111.

5. Anderson, 111.

6. Brad Sargent, *Godspace for the New Edge* (Cutting Edge Resources, Golden Gate Baptist Theological Seminary, 1997).

ABOUT THEOOZE.COM

TheOOZE exists to encourage the church to engage our emerging culture through relationships and resources. Our desire is to create environments where church leaders (traditional teachers and theologians as well as emerging storytellers/artists) can converse about and collaborate on resources and experiences for the broader faith community. We do this by providing places both online and offline for people to gather and communicate about how to live in the way of Jesus in our world.

Online, TheOOZE.com website offers a safe, authentic place where people can explore their faith in God, develop new global relationships, and be equipped to journey through life. Alongside our website, TheOOZE organizes the premiere annual event for the community, called Soularize: A Learning Party. At Soularize we strive to hold the tensions between creativity and information, theologians and artists, traditional and new voices.

Some of TheOOZE.com's core values include:

- See faith as a journey, not a destination
- Reintroduce the power of art
- Create experiential learning
- Take full advantage of technology
- Look to be surprised by nontraditional voices
- Promote collaboration and shared resources
- "Unpackage" rather than "repackage" theology

* Embrace the essence of the story of Christ
* Interact with the broadest network of faiths
* Widen our influence through use of the Internet
* Deepen our influence through face-to-face gatherings

TheOOZE is not connected with a particular church or denomination but reaches across various denominational lines, broad streams of Christianity, and beyond. We actively pursue content, resources, and relationships that are rooted in Protestant, Orthodox, and Catholic traditions. We seek to allow the various streams and traditions of Christianity the opportunity to highlight elements that they believe to be central to their expression of faith.

We know that some of our articles will directly contradict one another, and that's okay. We want to provide a place where people can explore new ways of thinking and new ways of connecting with God. We believe that an amazing tapestry will be woven together as we begin to come together for the purpose of new relationships and new forms of learning.

We invite you to join us at www.theooze.com.

ABOUT THE CURATOR

Spencer is a man of metaphors. "Kindling" describes his approach to speaking and consulting. He sparks new thought and conversation in his audiences and clients through his innovative thinking, humor, compassion, and use of arts and technology. Whether talking to ten or ten thousand, he encourages people to view their businesses and relationships in new ways, and they walk away ablaze with the possibilities.

"Cavepainting" is an ancient tool used to express the stories of the soul. Spencer has always been fascinated with individual and collective spiritual stories and has chronicled these through his photography. His work has been collected and exhibited at galleries, and he has taught photography at the university level. Spencer cofounded the Damah film festival exploring spiritual themes. In the 1990s, he created TheOOZE. com, a safe online community for a diverse faith-based population to connect through articles, message boards, and social networking. This community has grown to include over 250,000 monthly visitors from ninety countries. Spencer is author of *Making Sense of Church*, in which he contrasted his twenty-two years as a pastor in a traditional church with eight years of exploring emerging, nontraditional metaphors; and *A Heretics Guide to Eternity*, in which he explored the concepts of "who's in and who's out."

After achieving more than he dreamed as a teaching pastor at a megachurch, Spencer refocused on his original desires to love, serve, and live a grace-filled life. Spencer lives out his faith with what the *Los Angeles*

Times called "a church with no name." Spencer developed ETREK, collaborative learning groups that challenge the individual and traditional educational values. Soularize.net is his latest adventure, where he is looking for new ways to evolve.

Spencer lives with Lisa, his wife of twenty years, and children, Alden and Grace in southern California.

CHECK OUT THESE OTHER GREAT TITLES FROM THE NAVPRESS DELIBERATE LINE!

Chasing Francis

Ian Cron
978-1-57683-812-9
1-57683-812-9

Chase Falson has lost his faith—and he did it right in front of the congregation at his megachurch. Now the elders want him to take some time away. So Chase crosses the Atlantic, where he encounters the teachings of Francis of Assisi. Follow Chase's spiritual journey in the footsteps of Francis, and then begin one of your own through the pilgrim's guide included in this book.

Dangerous Faith

Joel Vestal
978-1-60006-197-4
1-60006-197-4

In *Dangerous Faith*, the idea of knowing God and spreading His matchless good news is challenged on the anvil of action: Will we simply talk about matters of compassion and justice on behalf of the world's marginalized people, or will we unite and become part of the Christ-hope and relief that changes the world one life at a time?

Daughters of Eve

Virginia Stem Owens
978-1-60006-200-1
1-60006-200-8

Is there something about being a woman that transcends time and cultural differences? This revised and updated version of *Daughters of Eve* examines both beloved and little-known heroines of the Bible. As you learn about them, you may be surprised at what you learn about yourself.

MORE GREAT TITLES FROM THE NAVPRESS DELIBERATE LINE!

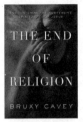

The End of Religion

Bruxy Cavey
978-1-60006-067-0
1-60006-067-6

The End of Religion contends that the Jesus described in the Bible never intended to found a new religion; instead he hoped to break down the very idea of religion as a way to God. With a fresh perspective on biblical stories, Cavey paints a picture of the world God originally intended and still desires: a world without religion.

The Year I Got Everything I Wanted

Cameron Conant
978-1-60006-145-5
1-60006-145-1

Paralleling the themes in the biblical book of Ecclesiastes, *The Year I Got Everything I Wanted* is poignant and provocative, heartbreaking and hilarious—a spiritual memoir that explores despair and pleasure with disquieting honesty.

COMING SOON!

Out of the Ooze: Volume 2

Spencer Burke

Out of the Ooze: Unlikely Love Letters to the Church from Beyond the Pew chronicled five years of the movement of the emerging church from critique to contribution at the grassroots level. *Out of the Ooze: Volume 2* will continue the chronicle but in near-real time—all articles submitted in the year 2007 will be considered for inclusion in the next book. Help us decide which articles should be included by reading, reviewing, and rating articles on TheOoze.com—or submit your own article for consideration. And, as before, all net proceeds will be donated.

To order copies, visit your local bookstore, call NavPress at 1-800-366-7788, or log on to www.navpress.com.

Environmental Benefits Statement

Active, holistic faith is the backbone of NavPress Deliberate books. We believe that every decision impacts the world of which God has charged us to be good stewards. We are good stewards when we care for people—from choosing to befriend a difficult next-door neighbor to volunteering at a homeless shelter. We are good stewards of the rest of creation by consuming resources wisely and in a way that also renews and blesses the world, its creatures, and its people. We believe in practicing what we publish, so all NavPress Deliberate books are "green." We have chosen to use paper products that do not contribute to deforestation in the world's poorest nations but instead reuse the waste produced by our own consumer culture. The chart below shows the positive impact this decision has on our environment this year.

	UNRECYCLED PAPER	DELIBERATE PAPER	DIFFERENCE
Wood Use	52 tons	26 tons	26 tons
Total Energy	575 million BTU's	450 million BTU's	125 million BTU's
Greenhouse Gases	85,353 lbs CO_2 equiv.	69,542 lbs CO_2 equiv.	15,811 lbs CO_2 equiv.
Wastewater	286,128 gallons	220,501 gallons	65,627 gallons
Solid Waste	34,175 pounds	25,748 pounds	8,427 pounds